Advance Praise

Trish Earnest's tumultuous journey is raw, moving and triumphant. Her bravely self-revelatory account of her battle with addiction will inspire many, as it inspires me. She is one badass survivor, not just of the disease of alcoholism, but of a flawed system that she is devoted to improving. A great read by an authentic new voice.

Maria Leonard Olsen, author of *Not the Cleaver Family—*
The New Normal in Modern American Families

blood on the walls is a gripping memoir that takes the reader through the throes of adolescent disaffection, alcoholism and addiction of a young girl. Trish begins her disaffection upon her family's move from Greece to the United States. She rapidly falls in with the crowd using drugs and alcohol to deal with the turmoil of adolescent life. Her story is one that takes the reader through an ineffective juvenile criminal justice system and its failure to improve the lives of those that it's designed to help. In spite of the significant trauma of her early years, she manages to become the committed mother of 2 boys, achieve sobriety and become a productive member of society. Truly a story of redemption in spite of a traumatic adolescence and adulthood. This story is highly recommended to anyone interested in both our juvenile justice system and its failures as well as the terrible scourge of alcoholism and drug addiction in our modern society and the ability to recover from this disease.

Bruce Eanet, Members Board of Trustees, Caron Treatment Centers

Quite the story! Many intense, disturbing, and poignant moments! Trish is an amazing survivor and really brings it home in this all too real and gritty memoir of addiction and of it's transcendence in recovery. I've heard many women speak of the role that the love of their children played in motivating their journey of healing, Trish nails it.

Jay Eubanks, LCSW-C, Psychotherapist at Psychological Solutions

blood
on the
walls

from rebellion to redemption

a memoir

TRISH EARNEST

ISBN: 1544265018
ISBN-13: 978-1544265018

Cover design and layout: Carol Earnest
Cover photo: Shutterstock
Author photo: Liezell Bradshaw

www.trishearnest.com

Dedicated to Tony and Max; I gave birth to you but in actuality, you gave me life.

ACKNOWLEDGEMENTS

There are so many people who supported me in the undertaking of this book. I spent hundreds of hours sitting in cafes, sandwich shops and home writing away painful memories that could not be spoken for decades. If nothing else, it was a cathartic process. Many will read this memoir and wonder why I could reveal such personal parts of my journey. The answer is simple; my story and experience will hopefully become wisdom and of value to others. It is my gift.

First and foremost I thank Tony and Max, my incredible sons who changed my whole perspective on life when they came in to this world. I love you to the moon. Thank you Joseph Scarnecchia, the father of my sons and my ex-husband. I love you dearly. I thank my sister Carol Earnest for her dedication and care that went into the cover, page layout and graphics of this book. You will always be my sweet little sister. Sheila, you were there for me in so many ways throughout the years. And you reminded me that God was there when I wasn't sure sometimes. Mom you NEVER gave up on me. Thank you. I love you more than you know. Dad, the life you gave us was magical. I thank you for the lessons and for being you. I will cherish the moments you held my hand. I love you.

I thank my two editors Jim Molis and Maria Leonard Olsen. Your support and feedback was critical and priceless. I could always count on you! You guided me in bringing this book to life. Finally, thank you Harlene Cohen Bernstein for your constant unconditional love.

ONE

Two lonely beds on metal stilts sat in the center of the bare room. A fluorescent ceiling lamp cast shadows on the small wooden table between the beds. The barred window overlooked a barren alley. The cold tile floor chilled my bare feet.

I spent the first hour or so unpacking, trying not to think of how I had come to be here, nor how I would pass the next 30 days. Then I reported to the front desk to be told what was on the schedule. Everyone was listlessly hanging around. Some patients were smoking.

One guy introduced himself immediately and started gabbing. "I'm Mickey. You're pretty. I've been here for a long time and I don't have that many friends. Do you have any smokes?"

"Sorry, don't have a lot of cigarettes right now," I answered.

It was difficult to take Mickey seriously. He sat hunched over on a couch and his fuzzy hair reminded me of a Brillo pad; it stuck out on the sides like a clown's, and the top was matted down with grease. He had pale skin with three or four days of stubble and a few pimples to punctuate his lack of self-care. His eyes struck me. They were beady, blue, and bloodshot. You could just see the emptiness behind them. He dressed like a nerd, with even less care than most. He wore a wrinkled, short-sleeved, plaid button-down shirt, which was tucked into the wrinkled, khaki pants that stopped short of his ankles, and black Keds.

The front desk consisted of half a doorway, open on the top where the medical staff administered medication and directions to the patients. It was locked so that patients couldn't harm the staff or access anything behind the doorway. Most of the staff was tolerable.

Of course they were bossy, and we were all less than sane in our present circumstances.

A dozen or so patients trickled in to get meds, smoke or wait for the next "activity" on the schedule. Today, apparently, I was to have group therapy in about five minutes.

Group therapy. What a joke! It was a great way for everyone to complain about being in the hospital. There were a few people that talked about why they were there: Family issues, problems with holding down a job, drinking too much. A few of them were just plain crazy; they didn't make any sense. Some were drooling.

Carly was in my group. She was a black woman in her mid-thirties. She had tried to tie her hair back, I could see, but it was nappy and flattened down from lack of care. She was not happy. She was also on a lot of meds. Carly's husband had put her in the hospital several months ago, and there was no telling when she would get out. Apparently, she was there because she wasn't caring for her children and was drinking too much. She had been found wandering the streets of D.C. one night while her young kids were home alone.

Shortly after "group" ended, I returned to my room. Soon, I had a visitor, who introduced himself as James. He was a young black man, maybe in his midtwenties. His hair was sort of an Afro, but pushed down on the sides from sleeping on it, and he wore a hospital gown. He was light skinned, with pockmarks on his face, and it was obvious he hadn't shaven. I was lying on my bed, and he slowly walked over, like a robot, with his arms guiding the way in front of him. I could hear the sound of his slippers sliding slowly on the cold floor. He was heavily medicated on Thorazine and his mouth was drooling.

"I've never kissed a white girl," he slurred. I was silent. There was dry crusted drool on the corners of his lips. It was disgusting. He leaned over and aimed for my mouth. I turned my head, and he kissed me on the cheek. I felt myself going into a paralysis mode. Again, he leaned down, and this time his lips touched mine. A putrid smell seeped from his body-- a mixture of urine, body odor and insanity. Immediately, I felt nauseated. I could feel no tears, no anger, no sorrow, just darkness.

Intellectually, I knew I had brought myself to this place, but emotionally there was a part of my heart and head that felt abandoned, unprotected. Now, involuntarily, I had entered a world where no one would watch over me, and I had no one to blame but myself. With a blank stare in his eyes, James slowly rose up and dragged himself back across the room. Again, his slippers slid along the vinyl tiled floor. The world seemed gloomy to me indeed.

Why on earth would my parents put me in this wretched place? I knew I wasn't crazy but here I was, the only minor on the psychiatric ward of George Washington University Hospital.

I had been in a rage and felt misunderstood, so I had turned to drugs and booze. I had been caught up in what had been done to me, and did not care how my actions had affected other people. I was falling deeper into a grotesque hole. The darkness that crept upon me as James left my room would eventually consume me, causing me to overlook many obstacles that were to come.

My childhood had been like a fairytale in which I had lived the "dream comes true" before I knew what a happy ending meant. My girlish mind could not conceive, nor appreciate, the lovely essence of my young days any more than it could picture the nightmares that lied ahead. Our family lived in one of the most beautiful lands of the world and reflected all of the outward appearances of happiness and success.

We frolicked on Mediterranean beaches, splashing in the salty water and sprinting on the soft sand. At home, I reveled in the glorious weather, playing with my sisters and whoever our friends were at the time, until Mom called us in for dinner. My favorite dishes were juicy meatballs with mint and thick French fries, and Mousaka, a Greek casserole with eggplant inside and fluffy béchamel on top. During the evenings when Dad wasn't "away" working, he would come home after dinner, sit with Mom and have a few martinis.

On Sundays, we had lunch together at the American Club after attending church. In the summer, my sisters, Nancy, Sheila, Carol and I often swam all day at the club, where all the families from the States would go and socialize. It was not extravagant or fancy but I loved jumping off the springboard and eventually became quite the graceful diver.

Exploring Mykonos with Mom's sister Martha.

As my sisters and I got older, there were summers when we would take a ferry to one of the remote islands to visit and explore. We passed several summers there in a rented house. Another year, we chartered a yacht and just sailed from one island to another as if the shimmery sea were our own. Or, we flew off to neighboring Rome or Paris.

It was a truly magical existence, of which I would not trade one moment. Indeed, it was so intoxicating that I would spend much of my life recklessly searching to recapture that fleeting bliss. Looking back, in many ways, it was my charming childhood that caused my traumatic adolescence because I was uprooted from what I felt then—and still does now—was my "real" home.

The fairytale ended when my family moved to the States from Athens on July 4, 1973, when I was 12 years old. I still recall how I never wanted that last flight to end, preferring instead to bounce among the puffy clouds as I had along the sandy Mediterranean shores.

In those days, there were no direct flights from Athens to Washington, D.C., where my father had been reassigned. Our flight had stopped over in New York first, and even though we were only in the airport my impression of the city was that of a dirty circus. It was loud, smoky and crowded. Everyone was rushing to get somewhere. It was worlds away from where I had departed.

Our family dogs, Cindy and Freckles, were miserable, being cooped up in traveling crates with the luggage. I remember Cindy in particular didn't seem to be doing well, for she was getting on in years at that point. We walked them a bit in New York and it was heart wrenching to put them back in the crates for the rest of the trip to D.C.

I had brought little keepsakes with me on the flight, stuffed in a Greek bag that my father had bought for me on the island of Mykonos. I had the Archie comic books that my sisters and I loved reading, as well as a select few shells and stones from my large collection that I had accumulated through the years. Some had been bought from shops or received as gifts but I had accumulated most of them on our excursions. Mom still has fond memories of me walking on the beach for hours, hunched down, as I searched for the most perfect shell.

Nestled in my traveling bag with some of these shells was quartz that I had found in the mountains above our Athens home. I loved how the crystals and quartz glistened a certain way in the light; it made my stones more enchanting. Somehow, all of these small tokens gave me comfort on my flights.

Back then we flew on Pan Am and the flights were luxurious. We always traveled first class because we were government officials. The crew was friendly and cared for our every need. Stewardesses would bring me and my sisters Pan Am souvenir bags stocked with tiny toys, foldable cups, and fuzzy socks for our feet. We were always given a cozy blanket and pillow. Once we all got settled on the plane it was like spending the night at a friend's house, only more exciting.

We had flown many times before returning to the States for good but each trip had been an adventure. Just getting to the airport and watching all the planes take off was a thrill. I still love the smell of airplane fuel because it brings back so many memories. It's like waking up on Easter morning as a child and you remember that "chocolate smell" from your Easter basket. The excitement of getting to the airport was familiar; checking luggage, waiting, boarding. We knew that soon we would take off to some thrilling place, either to another European country or to the States.

Though I paid scant attention to it at the time, I have since come to appreciate the largely thankless role that my mother played in these ventures, particularly when we were returning to the States for good. Moving was a constant in our lives but I know it was still hard for Mom getting all the packing for our return trip done and the house full of belongings boxed up. The government always sent movers to pack everything, but there were many details involved if you didn't want your valuables broken. Mom had to handle the house, the flights, moving arrangements, and our safety. Yet we were always tidy and dressed well, and everything seemed to get done without too many obstacles as far as I could tell.

We flew ahead of Dad so that we could find a house while he worked. My stomachache worsened as we drew closer to North

America and I clung to my seat after we landed in D.C. Given my father's work, we had flown into Dulles International Airport numerous times but I didn't feel any urgency to leave the plane this time, as everyone else bustled to get off.

I wished we were just visiting but we were "home" now.

⌘

Despite the fact that I had lived my entire life in Greece and Cyprus, we were heading to the States, which is where we would live now for an undetermined amount of time.

Born in Athens in 1961, I had grown up abroad, except for a three-year period in which we had lived in a quaint little neighborhood outside of Washington D.C., where all the children would collect lightning bugs together in the summertime. Everyone loved going to the swimming pool, hanging out for hours as the days drifted by.

A shopping center up the street from us had a five-and-dime store. A bunch of us kids would walk up together and buy bundles of candy for almost nothing. It was in the 1960s and long-haired hippies wearing headbands and tie-dyed t-shirts hung out in the parking lot, seemingly in their own world.

My sisters and I went to St. Jane de Chantal Catholic School, where I remember playing basketball with the nuns and having my First Holy Communion. There were many stories of the nuns being mean and heavy with the ruler on the back of the hand if you got out of order, but I do not recall experiencing that myself.

We then attended Grosvenor Elementary, which was a public school. It was during this time that my parents were struggling with Catholicism and the church's opposition to birth control. In 1968, Pope Paul VI issued Humanae Vitae, which declared use of birth control to be a sin. This declaration drove many liberal Catholics to defy the teachings of the church and we stopped attending mass regularly. I was too young to understand. As time went on, it was still confusing.

I became sick one Christmas during that stay in America. I had Scarlet Fever and Grandma Earnest came to watch over me while my parents and sisters went to a party. I joked about how I was too weak to open my presents that year.

We would visit our relatives on holidays and some weekends. We spent many Sundays at Grandma Earnest's house and she always served ham, Brussels sprouts, and potatoes. I didn't care for Brussels sprouts and there would always be a sour odor as we walked in the house. But Grandma Earnest always had ginger ale, which became an all-time favorite.

Grandma Earnest visiting us in Olympia.

Those three years remain patchy in my mind, although I do recall making several good friends that I stayed in touch with for awhile. And I remember that Dad was home regularly, which was not always the case in Greece. There was a "friendly" feeling about the neighborhood; people looked out for each other and did things together. All the kids would gather to play hide and seek. I recall one night when I was "it" and I was on the lookout for everyone as I climbed over a fence. On the other side was a German shepherd that took a good bite at my ankle. Funny, but it didn't change my affection for animals.

For the most part, I had happy memories of those two years stateside.

So here we were, after four years of living abroad again, returning to the States, this time seemingly for good. Mom gathered us as best she could before exiting the plane. Nancy, at that point, had long, dark blond hair and fine facial features. She was thin and usually on the quiet side during adolescence; and at 14 years old seemed to take being the oldest seriously. A year younger, Sheila had lighter hair than Nancy and lots of freckles. She seemed a bit tomboyish but was always the smarter one. Carol, 9, was going through a tough time then with her thick glasses and braces; but she was always so adorable and had her long, beautiful hair that everyone envied.

My hair was very blonde and long, past my shoulders. I never knew what to do with it since normally my mom kept it short as a younger girl. At 12 years old at the time, I still had my girlish cuteness but was at that odd, pre-adolescent age, where my face and body were changing.

I did not want to get off that plane for this final destination. We were all working our way up the aisle, slowly. The crew was thanking everyone for "flying Pan Am." I felt sick. I could feel the air outside before I approached the door.

I still remember the air. The humidity hugged my face and lungs so tightly that it took me a few minutes to become acclimated. I have since heard that the air in Athens is now humid due to the pollution, but it was not like that when we lived there. Summertime heat in Washington, D.C., was foreign to me, and the thick oxygen was difficult to endure. There also was a moist, wormy smell, so it must have just rained before we landed.

Of the numerous times I had arrived at Dulles, this landing felt different. We slowly descended the metal steps that had been rolled up to the plane. Each foot fall reverberated in my head. I felt ill.

Everyone was maneuvered onto a shuttle bus that took us to the main terminal, where we would wait in line to go through Customs. Mom was patient and focused with all of us, as if we were little chicks and she the mother hen that was keeping us in line. She flashed frustration and anger at some of the most trying times, but was resolute in her efforts, having grown accustomed to shepherding us on these Trans-Atlantic expeditions. Fatigue inevitably set in though, as we waited for our luggage.

We were greeted by Mom's parents, the Hoehns, and Dad's mother, Grandma Earnest. They were ecstatic, but I did not return the warmth of their embraces. We had seen them so little over the years that they were like strangers.

It took two cars to get us all loaded up and over to Grandma Earnest's house, where we would stay until Mom found a house for us. This was marvelous for me, staying in the house where Dad grew up. It was in Bethesda, off of River Road. It was a big, brick house with a large front lawn, atop a hill like many of the neighboring homes. Huge, leafy trees shaded all of the houses in the aging neighborhood. Gigantic bushes of white, pink, red, and purple azaleas sprung from the lawns.

Grandma Earnest was about five feet tall and thin. She was British. She had beautiful silky skin, her hair was gray and she would go to the beauty parlor to have it curled. She had thick glasses and always wore a dress midway past her knees, with little, chunky heels.

From as far back as I can remember Grandma Earnest looked old. Her husband had died when my father was 12 years old, and she had lived alone for many years. She preferred privacy and was usually antsy, especially when Dad wasn't around.

Mom found a place for us to live in Rockville, Maryland. I adjusted to the schools and neighborhood with few problems. I made friends and did OK in school. My best friend, Cathy, lived right across the street, and we spent a lot of time together. We would walk to a nearby shopping center just to hang out or to get an ice cream. We also went to movies together, such as "Young Frankenstein" and "Blazing Saddles," and had sleepovers.

Mom, Carol, Nancy, me, Dad, and Sheila posing on a jungle gym in Rockville, Maryland.

Carol didn't fare as well with the move from Greece to Rockville. She was having trouble in school and transferred twice within a year. Nancy and Sheila seemed okay, and each had a few friends.

There were woods and a creek down the street from us, and a bunch of the neighborhood kids would get together and build forts. We could spend all day amongst those trees.

In our first year home, I spent two weeks away at Camp Waredaca in the summer. It was a typical, young adolescent experience that I cherished. We slept in cottages, rode horses and swam in a big lake when the days were sizzling hot. There was a huge dining hall that all the campers would congregate in for meals.

We would groom the horses and ride them for hours; learning to trot and gallop. There were special excursions where we could take the horses on overnights and camp hours away from the cabins.

Some nights, we would have big bonfires, roast hot dogs and marshmallows, and sing songs or tell ghost stories. Some of us played innocent pranks on our fellow campers. We would hide some of their belongings or toothpaste their pillows. It seems there was always a bit of a devilish side to me. I had innocent girlish feelings for a boy, but we were there for such a short time that nothing transpired, and he and I never kept in touch.

After a year in Rockville, we needed to move again. Dad had been driving into his headquarters in Langley, Virginia, for emergency calls at night, and he was not close to work. Mom and Dad contemplated moving to Bethesda or Potomac, as the quality of the schools were better there than where we were living and it was a shorter drive to Langley. It was decided we would move to Potomac.

I had grown weary of moving by now, and I believe it affected Nancy, Sheila and Carol in various ways as well. I never settled. Even when we lived overseas, there were constant shifts. Friendships were temporary. Some had actually lasted three or four years during our last stay in Greece, but such bonds were few and far between.

I yearned for those Mediterranean days, of which I had regaled the kids in Rockville with tales of the isles that I had visited and the villages in which I had grown up. I longed for the "normalcy" that we had left behind and sought desperately to replicate it Stateside. Yet there were no family sojourns to the beach, or exciting excursions to exotic locales. Dad was not sweeping us off on thrilling adventures. It seemed as if there was nothing to look forward to, just suburban drudgery. The happy ending that I had lived had dissipated into a dreary reality.

TWO

I was 14 years old when we moved to Potomac in 1975, and I practically convulsed upon entering Cabin John Junior High School. The guidance counselor had a cheerleader show me around and she introduced me to her haughty groupie friends. They all gave me snide looks. My clothes were different, my hair was not snazzy and I still wore braces. Most of the kids that went to Cabin John Junior High also had grown up together. I was the new kid, the weird kid.

Socially, I was a disaster. By no means were we paupers, but there was a competitiveness in this elite community that I had never experienced. It thrived on materialism and image. Ill-prepared and insecure, I didn't measure up. I would sit alone in the cafeteria and all the kids would gawk at me as if I were on display. Their glances felt like daggers. A group of boys gave me a cruel nickname. At first, it was subliminal and I wasn't aware of the humor at my expense, but it was obviously meant to hurt. And it did. They called me "horse".

School was stressful academically, as well. I'd gone to so many different schools while we moved around that I just didn't have a consistent education. I felt inadequate and my grades had suffered.

I couldn't imagine how my sisters, Nancy, Sheila, and Carol were all dealing with our latest move. At least Nancy and Sheila were in high school together, so in a sense, they had each other. Carol was in elementary school, so puberty hadn't kicked in, but I knew it was tough for her too. She wore braces and headgear to fix her teeth, and thick glasses to remedy her "stray eye." While we lived in Greece, Mom would take her to specialists in Germany and at one point I think there was talk of Carol possibly needing surgery. For several years Carol had to wear a patch over her eye. She was such a beautiful girl and I believe this took a lot of her spirit and confidence away.

Where I had come from, life was carefree. I didn't care if I was popular or not. My wish was to be anywhere else than Potomac, Maryland. I didn't want to play this game. But no one seemed to understand my dilemma so I kept to myself. How could I tell Mom and Dad? What would they do about it anyway?

I had brought two pet rabbits from our Rockville home and Dad had helped build a fenced-in area for them, with a pen to protect them from the elements. One morning I went out to feed my little bunnies some lettuce and carrots. Both of them were bleeding from multiple holes. I ran to get my parents. Dad immediately recognized that the holes were from BBs. It broke my heart to find my pets in such a state, but they were alive!

We took the rabbits to a vet and he said they would be fine. The veterinarian removed some of the BBs; there were about six in each one of the rabbits. Eventually, my pets escaped and we hoped that they thrived better out in the wild than they did in captivity. I never knew who had shot them, or why.

Around this time, I started developing excruciating headaches. At times, all I could do was lay in bed with the lights off, waiting for the pain to subside. Mom took me to several doctors and I was diagnosed with migraines. One physician prescribed powerful pain relievers that knocked me out. We then we went to a specialist who practiced biofeedback, a process that involves measuring one's blood pressure, body temperature and muscle tension. Basically, I was hooked up to a non-invasive machine and was taught to try and gain control of these bodily functions. Easier said than done, especially when suffering physically, and emotionally.

Not long after, Sheila also fell victim to migraine headaches, only hers were with aura, meaning she would have little or no pain but would be dizzy, see flashes of color and struggle to speak clearly. She had trouble speaking at school one day and Mom was called right away to take her to the doctor. They thought she had been taking illegal drugs. Mom was livid! I believe Sheila had one other such episode in her adolescence.

⊞

One day in the school cafeteria, a group of girls came up to me: Tara, Alison, and Joan. They seemed friendly enough. They weren't all dolled up like the phony cheerleaders. Nor did they give me the snotty look or attitude that I had received earlier. I began to sit with them at lunch, which was a welcomed change from eating alone, and we eventually became friends. I joined their clique. Life seemed to be on the upswing.

Tara had blonde hair, blue eyes, and was about my height. She had a bubbly personality that I liked. Alison was tall, with black hair and brown eyes. She was pretty, but always talked about how ugly she was. After a while, Tara and Alison were my two best friends. Sometimes they walked home after school with me, and we would hang out at my house and just talk. My parents liked them, and as time went by, I became more social.

One Friday night, a small group of us went to a party at the house of a girl named Molly. Alison and Tara came to get me, and we all walked over together. As we got close to Molly's house, I could hear music from down the road. Molly greeted us at the door. She seemed glad that I had come. We went downstairs, and when everybody saw me, they gave me odd looks. I had seen most of these people in school, but I didn't know most of them. My initial reaction was to turn and run out the door but I stayed.

There was a musky smell. I could see people smoking cigarettes, but there was something else. When I reached a small doorway and saw Molly, I realized she was smoking a pipe. It was pot. Everybody was stoned!

Marijuana was a mystery to me at the time. My sisters and I had no exposure to drugs while living in Europe. Molly asked me if I wanted a "hit" off the pipe, and I told her that I had never smoked pot before. She said, "Well, if I show you how to do it, will you try it?" I replied with, "I guess so." I was certainly curious.

The first time I tried it, I coughed, and everybody started laughing. After awhile, I took a puff without half my lungs coming out, and I started feeling different. It felt like my body was swaying back and forth and I was floating. I couldn't stop giggling. Everything and everyone appeared soft. The music blared in my ears, but the vibration boomed all the vile thoughts out of my brain. The sensation was like no other I had ever experienced. I liked it.

It was getting late, and I had to go home despite my wanting to stay longer. The walk through the neighborhood was strange; it was as if I were in a movie. I felt like I was moving in slow motion and all the houses looked fuzzy. I wanted to stop and lie in the grass and stare at the sky forever. If only time could have stood still.

When I got home, my parents asked me a lot of questions about the party. I told them I had a great time and that I was tired. I kissed them goodnight and went to bed.

The next afternoon after school, I tried pot again. It quickly became a habit. Everybody would skip classes and go to a place called "the hill" to get high. I would go home and sit in front of the TV in the family room. Every noise was an echo. I was giggly. My Mom looked weird. She wanted to know if I was okay. I'd say I was fine.

My mouth would get dry. I would get the "munchies," have a snack, and then go to my room to nap. When I went to school the next day, everybody would be on the hill again, smoking pot, so I would get high too. I loved it. It was as if I had hopped a plane and flown to heaven. I was now amongst those clouds from which I never wanted to descend.

Smoking pot and hanging out with this accepting crowd opened a joyful horizon for me. Getting stoned relieved the pain and solitude that had built up inside. My heart had been cracking a little more each day and only the drugs mended the damage. Yes, it was that simple; all it took was any possible diversion from the asphyxiating well of despair I was falling into. I had found my remedy.

Before long, I was going to a lot of parties and getting stoned every weekend. I took up cigarette smoking as well. I thought I was "cool." I tried to quit but couldn't. I was hooked on nicotine and my habit soon turned into a pack a day. When I would have friends over to my house and we would smoke in my room, I had incense burning to camouflage the smell. Mom thought it was so nice that I was burning this pretty fragrance upstairs.

At one of the parties, several people were drinking beer and I wanted to try. I vividly remembered the taste from when I was a little girl. My parents would play tennis at the American Club in Athens, and then sit and have beer and Greek caviar, otherwise known as taramousalata. They would let me take innocent sips. I loved the bubbly liquid going down my throat. It actually quenched my thirst. There was no "feeling" I could associate with sipping that beer, but I distinctly remember sheer delight in its taste. So, drinking came easily to me as a teenager.

I soon started skipping school. I wanted an escape and it seemed that the people I gravitated toward were the ones who needed a similar outlet. We could all be screw-ups together. Back then, we were called the "Freaks."

Into the middle of the school year, I developed a crush on Dillon. He was adorable and on the soccer team. Dillon had long, wavy hair that he would always flip to the side with his thumb. He had a wide smile and his face was sprinkled with Irish freckles. His glittery blue eyes seemed so inviting, so warm. He was one of the better soccer players and I loved the sport from growing up in Europe. Tara decided that she "liked" Dillon too. But soon Dillon and I started "going out." It seemed that he actually had some feelings for me. He was sweet and never treated me disrespectfully. We lasted a few months and it was an innocent relationship.

Interestingly, other boys would call me and ask me out. I didn't have any experience with the opposite sex. One popular boy, who will remain nameless, wanted to meet for an impromptu rendez-vous. I snuck out late on a school night and ran to meet him at a trailer near the school grounds. Nameless was there when I arrived. The trailer was filled with smoke. He had a tall bong and had been getting high while he had waited.

Nameless was a tall, bulky Jewish stud with a big nose. I thought he was cocky as hell and so-so looking. He was extremely popular with everyone in the school so I was flattered when he called. He generously offered me numerous bong hits and I got high. Then we started making out, which initially was okay. He took his shirt off, and mine. We touched each other. I could not look him in the eyes; I was disconnected from this event. Then Nameless grabbed my hand and maneuvered it down toward his crotch. He wanted me to undo his pants. I didn't want to. What would I do after they were undone? How awkward! Together, we unzipped his jeans and unbuckled his belt. Nameless pulled down his pants and a floppy penis sprung out. He put my hand on it. I had no idea what to do; I didn't even know what an erection was. The male anatomy was a total mystery. My only saving grace was that it was dark in that trailer.

So here was Nameless, wanting me to stimulate his pubescent flesh. Feeling obligated, I continually put my hand on his penis and ran my fingers up and down, but beyond that, I had no idea what he desired. Nameless did not appear to be frustrated and eventually pulled his pants back up. This was much to my relief. We did a few more bong hits and called it a night.

A few weeks later, Nameless called and wanted to meet again. Did he like me? Again, I took it as a compliment. I snuck out by going down the stairs quietly and slowly, one by one on my butt. Even the dog slept through my fleeing for a tryst. As soon as I got out the side door, I ran out into the moonlight along the side of the house, then quickly into shrubbery so that I couldn't be seen.

Nameless was there just like the first time. I was a tiny bit excited to see him. He had his bong again and the smoke invited me into the trailer. He took me into his arms and gave me a peck on the lips. I was taken aback by all of this. Together, we got high and made small talk. Then Nameless wanted me to undo his jeans again—AND mine. Together we undid our pants and pulled them down to our feet, almost methodically. Nameless wanted to touch me. I let him. He kissed me and touched me inside. His breathing was getting heavy and his body was moving rather aggressively toward mine. I don't think I was nervous, but I wasn't sure if I was prepared for what was to come.

This testosterone-driven young man continued to grab my hand and direct it to his genitals. He must have known that I knew nothing about his male adolescent boner. Interestingly, he had me wrap my fingers around his penis and run them up and down. I'm sure it was not extremely exciting for Nameless, but it certainly was a grand lesson for me. That same night, Nameless touched me and felt me. I was young and inexperienced; I didn't find it arousing per se. But here I was with a boy that was popular in the school who actually showed interest in me for reasons that were still mysterious. We met one other night after that. As far as I knew, Nameless never said anything to the other kids about our secret rendezvous.

After we settled in Potomac, my parents were glad when I began making a lot of friends. But then they noticed a drastic change in my behavior and attitude. Within six months or so, I was not talking to them much, and they were asking me a lot of questions.

At school I started ending up in the principal's office. It seems I was an anomaly to Cabin John Junior High. Initially, they gave me detention. Big deal! Realistically, I couldn't keep up with what was going on in class, so in a way, I was saving face. I would just gaze out the window while the teacher would lecture, wishing I was anywhere else but in that class. Academically I had digressed and my grades were dropping. Detention quickly became common.

My friends and I would go the health suite and pretend that we were sick. Sometimes we would put a lighter to the thermometer and the nurse would say, "Wow, you have a high temperature!"

There was one disastrous occasion when a group of us drank at school. A few of us got hold of some booze from our parents' liquor cabinets and brought it in to school. By noon we were obliterated. We couldn't find our friend Joan and we madly searched the school. Finally, one or two of us, who were still drunk, found her behind the curtains of the stage in the gym. She was completely passed out! We were frantic. I don't think at that moment we realized how frightening a situation it was and the immense trouble we were in.

Molly, Tara and I rushed to the office and the receptionist called 911. The ambulance came and rushed Joan to the hospital. She had to have her stomach pumped. Her parents wouldn't let her see any of us after that. She wouldn't even talk to us at school. She would act subdued. It was bizarre. All of us were suspended.

Mom and Dad first found out about my getting high from Nancy. I felt betrayed by her about this, because we had been close until that point. I thought I could trust her. Mom said later that there were friends from Greece over at the house for cocktails, and they were all chit-chatting. The friends were relieved that none of their children had turned to drugs. Mom and Dad expressed the same feeling. Apparently, Nancy overheard the conversation. She told Mom she begged to differ, and then told her about me. Unfortunately, after that, my relationship with Nancy changed dramatically.

Unbeknownst to my friends, teachers, and parents, I also was befriending the janitors. Anytime I wanted to, I could go into their back office discreetly and drink with them. There was always a bottle of something, usually whiskey, and sometimes even a joint. As odd as it sounds, there was an ear to talk to. They honestly felt like kindred souls in my life at the time. These men genuinely cared about me and never acted inappropriately in any way. It was a confidential relationship.

My parents were distraught. They had no idea how to handle a teenage daughter on drugs and booze, not to mention the combative attitude that I was developing. I was demonstrating demonic behavior. They could not comprehend what was going on, what had become of me. They started talking to other parents for support and possible ideas. They would "check" me when I came home. Mom noticed my red eyes and smelled smoke.

Consequently, my parents and I began getting into aggressive confrontations over my repulsive attitude. I heard there was a group of parents meeting at each other's homes, and they watched films on what kids were like "under the influence." This was the ultimate embarrassment to me! All communication had broken down.

Mom and Dad issued restrictions, but I would not adhere to any rules and became more and more rebellious. They would sit me down and ask me questions. It was becoming more strained between us, until finally they said that I would be going to a psychiatrist to find out what was "wrong." This would be the first of many psychiatrists that they would try.

Though I did not know it at the time, Mom would stay up worrying about me when I was out all night. Was I alive? Was I warm? Overdosing? Why wouldn't I come home? Dad would drive around looking for me, including at one of the bars that he had heard we frequented. No one could reach me; I was turning cold. One psychiatrist diagnosed me with a "dual personality." Mom was furious at him for saying this; she thought it was damaging.

Years later I would find out that Mom and Dad had been ostracized from our neighborhood. Nobody wanted to be associated with them because they had a daughter who used drugs. It must have humiliated them and my sisters.

Meanwhile, Dad had gotten an overseas assignment offer. Mom was terrified that if he took it and I was on drugs, it would be devastating for me to move to another country. So, Dad requested to put himself "on hold" for family reasons, explaining that he had a daughter who was having some difficulties.

In fact, I was already an addict and an alcoholic. I had embarked on a new life, ingesting anything to tune out.

THREE

One day at school, Christine asked me if I wanted to get high. There was something edgy about Christine, but still she seemed all right. It was mid-afternoon and we decided to go to Potomac Village to get some beer or liquor. I was skipping class anyway, so we hitchhiked.

Back then there were only two gas stations and two tiny lineups of stores in the Village. I had only been there a few times before with my mother and sister, who would get supplies from the horse supply store. Nancy was an avid rider and later attended an elite equestrian school.

Christine got a stranger to buy us a six-pack of beer. We then went into the woods behind Drug Fair to drink three each. As we were walking to get something to eat, I found myself stumbling. I wasn't drunk, but I was buzzed.

Christine introduced me to some of the Potomac kids that she knew. They were quite a litter. Lee, who was Christine's older brother, had long brown hair, a mustache, and glasses like John Lennon's. At 19, he was into hard drugs. He didn't like smoking pot, but was often drunk if he couldn't get smack (heroin). Billy, 20, had jet-black hair that was always shiny, penetrating black eyes, and was part American Indian. Christine said he got into fights and had already done a few stints in jail for assault. Marie, 17, was Billy's girlfriend and had been for about three years. She was Greek, had medium length, wavy brown hair, big green eyes, and was a little on the heavy side. After school let out for the summer, I started hitchhiking up to Potomac to meet everybody. It was then that I started getting into angel dust

(PCP) and pills. Dust literally fries your brain cells but users don't think about that when they are getting high. When I smoked it, I never knew what was going to happen. Sometimes it made me hallucinate, other times I felt like I was in space. I recall one episode when I was with Lee and we had been smoking dust while we were on our way to a party. I was standing outside in the dark, trying to run inside but my feet would not move. Another time we were in Lee's car driving to the Village and I swear it seemed like the cars coming the other way were driving right through us. But bad highs like these never scared me away from chasing the good ones.

One day, I had been escorted to my locker by a teacher and the vice principal of the school; back then there was no such thing as security in schools. Someone has informed the office that I had drugs in my locker, 100 hits of codeine and morphine. I had gotten them from someone in the older crowd to sell or take. I was suspended for 2-3 days. Mom didn't understand why I was doing drugs and drinking. She had no idea the torment I had gone through at school when we moved to Potomac. I knew I was in a lot of trouble at home because of the discovery of the drugs in my locker. I packed some things and ran away—just went right out the door. I went to my friend Alison's house, and her parents let me stay there for about a week.

Alison's dad was a famous, reputable psychiatrist who at the time was the director of mental health for the National Institute of Medical Health. Her mom was a beautiful woman who stayed home and read a lot. I think in their own way, they thought they could help me, especially Alison's dad. There would be meetings between them and my parents –- always unsuccessful.

I remember Alison buying me lots of Peppermint Patties because they were my favorites. We would stay up at night and listen to "Bohemian Rhapsody" and just talk. That song still brings back memories of being at Alison's. And there was the song "Desperado" by the Eagles, too. It rang true for me in some way. Alison's sisters also were fun. They would hang out with us when we were high, even though they were straight.

Alison and I would get high and go for walks in the neighborhood. At the time, getting high was working. All my troubles disappeared once I took a toke off that joint. The only problem was that my pain still existed. It only passed from my mind temporarily.

Late one afternoon, my mother came to pick me up from Tara's house, and I had a bong wrapped in my jacket. Mom knew I had something. She kept asking, "What's in the jacket, Patricia?" I would tell her, "Nothing!" She stopped the car and tried to grab the jacket. We wrestled for several moments until I finally threw it at her and ran. When I looked back, Mom was chasing me, with a primal scream, "You get back here you little bitch!" She kept hollering, "I'm going to kill you!" I ran through the woods and got lost. The whole time, Tara's dog had followed me. I knew Mom was looking for me and that she was still blazing mad. So I stayed in the woods.

Finally, I reached Alison's house. I was dirty and upset. I told her what had happened, and she said that my father had called. Dad said it would be best if I stayed at Alison's until my mother and I calmed down. When Dad came over, he wanted me to go see my psychiatrist. So I went. I hated going to the shrink. I didn't want to talk. I had no say over anything. I had no control.

I stayed at Alison's for about a week, until my father decided I should return home. I still felt hassled, and my Mom still searched my room. She also would search my pockets when I came home and smelled my body. It was invasive.

I tried to control my life by repeatedly running away, only to inevitably return. My parents were never horrible to me, but I could not help bucking their constraints. Mom and Dad wanted me to stay in my room, but I wanted to flee. Mom policed me constantly. My sisters were angry with me and wouldn't talk to me. No one knew or cared how miserable my life had become in our dreadful town. Whenever I did get out of the house, I didn't want to come home, so I would call and say that I was going to stay out. Then I would stay at a friend's house. I left the house when I chose to and did what I wanted to do.

Mom and I clashed frequently. She had a temper. I had a monstrous chip on my shoulder. When my sisters and I were little, Mom had yelled at us and spanked our bottoms. When we used "naughty" words, she had cleaned our mouths out with soap. But now that I was older—and usually either under the influence of drugs or booze, or "coming down" from something—Mom raged. We argued. Yelled. Slapped. Soon we were rolling on the floor, kicking and punching. It was pitiful. It accomplished nothing.

Somehow I got wind of Southern Comfort during this time. I delighted in this elixir as it went down my throat easily, and it made me warm in the wintertime. It reminded me of the medicine that Mom would rub on my gums when I was sick. Southern Comfort made me drunk quickly because it had high alcohol content and it gave me a great buzz. My older friends could get Southern Comfort for me from the liquor store. Getting what I wanted, whether it was drugs or booze didn't seem to be much of an inconvenience at all.

My friends and I would go to the bars. IDs weren't a problem for me, and a 16-year-old getting into a bar was not much of an issue. We loved to drink and dance in those establishments. I didn't have a care in the world. I was accepted as part of a crowd. They embraced me as their "Angel." Because I was so young, they were looking after me in a dysfunctional way. If there was a problem with a man in a bar, someone would protect me. I liked the feeling that someone was watching my back.

There was a place in Potomac Village at that time called the Happy Pickle. A total dive, it served beer, burgers, greasy steak-and-cheese subs, and not much else. They served everything in a plastic red basket with thin, waxy paper under your food. When we hadn't eaten in a day or more, the subs tasted so good that it didn't matter how much fat dripped from your fingers onto the waxy paper. We all went to the Happy Pickle to play pinball or Pac Man. Pac Man had just come out and people were going crazy over the game. But I liked pinball, and was good. My friend, Billy, showed me how to shake the machine or hit it with my hip just right so that the ball would go where I wanted it to roll.

Sometimes there was a small bunch of us that would go to the Chinese restaurant in the Village. It was usually Christine, her brother Lee, and a few others. The owner hated us. Usually we would go in barefoot and our feet would be black. We didn't think it was that big of a deal. They would serve us quickly, and we would be gone just as fast. Often we would get the food to go. After awhile, the owner told us that we couldn't eat in the restaurant.

I knew my reality was different now. I couldn't cope with my life in the present. My anger was unleashed. I was consumed by sorrow and loneliness. My only answer at the time was to escape further into my world of drugs and booze.

FOUR

I missed Greece immensely. It had been my native land.

I missed spending the summers on secluded islands, swimming in the Mediterranean Sea. How I longed for the aqua blue ocean, our tiny village and the warm people that we had grown to love.

I had known nothing but the beauty and delight of the sparkly, transparent ocean; the delicate sea breeze brushing my skin; the city of Athens and all the little villages and sites that we would visit regularly. All of it was gone, taken from me forever.

My family had spent several summers on the island of Aegina with friends. Just like the other isles, the houses and buildings were white-washed, contrasted with blue shutters or shingles. It was so Greek!

We would walk along the dirt road that didn't allow cars. Some of the Greeks had donkeys. I remember passion flowers that would hang from vines on little fences along the way to the beach; they were the most glorious flowers, with deep purple petals. We would snorkel and find delicate shells for our collections. All day long we would have the shore to ourselves, to splash around and to dive to the bottom of the sea. Occasionally, someone would find a beautiful starfish and yell out as if they had won a prize. We would also jump from big rocks and boast about who the best diver was. It was all ours.

At dusk, we would walk into the town to gather our food that had been baked in the wood-fired oven all day. There was no electricity or running water on the island, but that was fine with us.

When we got a whiff of the juicy lemon and oregano chicken and potatoes, our mouths would water all the way back to the house. Everyone would dig in and tell tales of who dove down the furthest for the shells or sea urchins that day.

View from the summer house on the island of Aegina.

Summer house on Aegina, no running water or electricity.

Dad would come on the weekends. On those nights, the men would build fires for all the kids to sit around and roast marshmallows. We would play charades and tell jokes. The mornings welcomed us with the smell of the salty ocean and the vision of deep blue in the distance. Always, there was a delicate breeze like a song in the air.

We had a huge ice block in the fridge to keep the food cold. There was a gypsy woman who would come around on her donkey selling the ice that we used frequently. The bathroom was an outhouse. During the day, we would get water from a well. All of us would take turns fetching water. It was part of the primitive life of the island; we embraced it. Honestly, you could stand on the tip of any island and become intoxicated for hours by the tapestry of sights, smell and sounds.

There were annual wine festivals that we would all go to as a family. All the wine was in large, wooden barrels with spouts, and you were given a little glass and carafe when you entered the festival. Even as children, we could taste the wine and fill our carafes. By the end of the evening all the Greeks and anyone else present would be quite merry. Music would blare. Laughter was everywhere. Lamb roasting on a spit smelled heavenly. People were dancing, sailing around in a gigantic circle, with everyone holding hands giggling joyously. We would all indulge in tender, juicy meat, crisp salads with tangy goat cheese, and fresh, soft, bread. The Greeks would throw plates to the floor, and the men would put the children on their shoulders as they danced. It was exhilarating!

Life was simple and uncomplicated when we lived in Greece. We were insulated. We just didn't realize how much so until we got to the States. Obviously, things would have been different if we had been better prepared for what lay ahead of us. Perhaps I never would have had the troubles that I did, had I not been uprooted so suddenly. But how were Mom and Dad to know?

Eating at the taverna in Mykonos with another family.

We lived in Cyprus for two years when we were first stationed abroad. Dad had to go ahead of us six months beforehand to secure our stay amidst bombings and inter-communal fighting between the Greeks and Turks, who continue to divide Cyprus between them today. My sister says that our maid at the time was from the Turkish side and that we would hide her in the trunk of our car to keep her from Greeks.

Of course, at the time we were stationed there, I was too young to fully grasp the surrounding violence. United Nations security forces escorted us from the Turkish side to Nicosia, on the Greek side where we lived. Dad spoke fluent Greek, and we were all acquiring the language.

I was little when we lived in Cyprus and mostly remember trips to the beach, and Dad being busy at work. I also recall a delicacy we all favored: Greek bread with butter and sugar sprinkled on top.

I have lasting memories of the days when we lived in the village of Kiffisia, in the mountains above Athens. At night, so many stars gleamed in the sky that they were like jewels that went on forever. In Kiffisia, we could venture into the city without worry. We would ride the train into Monastaraki, the flea market, and stay all day. We knew nothing of drugs or "bad" people. There were no cliques at our schools, just all of us Americans. We were like our own society within this lovely country. Everyone knew each other, and the Greeks were friendly and gracious. Everywhere we went in Greece we were welcomed, even though we stuck out because Mom had four girls and all of us were blonde in a sea of dark-haired people.

In Kifissia with my sisters waiting for the school bus a block from our house.

Dad said we were like celebrities; the Greeks would come up to us and pinch our cheeks and want to touch our blonde hair. At one point, Mom cut my hair short and I felt like a little boy. She said it tangled up "like a bird's nest" and that I should be thankful that I didn't have to wear a bathing cap in the swimming pool. But I missed my long, lush, hair.

Occasionally, we would go to dinner with Mom and Dad, to one of the many restaurants with the customary grape vines hanging over trellises. Heavenly whiffs came from the kitchens. Greek music played. People were happy. Often, we ate outdoors and most of the traditional theatres were outside as well. Sometimes, my sisters and I would chase after the horse carriages and hitch a ride on the back. The carriage driver hardly ever knew, and if he did, we would just get yelled at, rather good-naturedly.

Kiffisia was a small but elegant village. It was laid-back and easygoing. The major intersection in town had no stoplight, so a police officer would direct traffic. At Easter time, he would sit in a big decorated "egg." He looked hilarious! All the bakery shops would stack up these delectable powdered cookies, called kourabiedes, in the windows. The desserts were something we would venture out for some nights as a treat. We would get rich, creamy chocolate filled tortes or delicately, moist, layered mocha cakes.

The drivers were crazy! If they got angry at each other, they would stop in the middle of the road and proceed to yell and cuss at each other; hands and arms would swing in the air only. They would spew their anger out in words, inflate their egos a bit, and then be on their way. That would be the end. No violence.

We camped often in our VW bus.

The hills steeped as you drove further up the mountain. Dad would joke with us and stop in the middle of the street with the Volkswagen Camper, which had a manual transmission. He would pretend that we were rolling down the hill backwards and that he couldn't stop. I liked it when Dad kidded around with us.

We sometimes drove our VW onto an isolated beach and stayed one or two nights. The Camper had a sink, fridge and hammock bed that came out when the room popped up. There was a bed that unfolded in the back. We nestled on the shore and woke to the soothing waves and smell of the sea.

A gypsy camp was down the street from us. The roosters would awaken us early in the morning. And, every now and then, we would get a ring on the doorbell and one of the gypsies would be begging for money. Or, several of them would come to the door and ask to play their bongos or fiddles for money. Occasionally, a donkey or sheep would wander into our yard. We would just shepherd it back.

Nancy, me, and Sheila. We rescued stray animals found discarded in the nearby ditch.

Our house was enormous! It had been a headquarters for the Germans during the war and remained vacant years after we moved out. But we made the most of the cavernous home in the meantime, even roller skating on the large, flat roof. The gardens were so big that Mom had a gardener. But she loved to be out there herself tending to flowers, pruning away. The roses were gorgeous. It was similar to an English garden with a path that crisscrossed through it. We had a fig tree and a cherry tree that we would climb. In the spring, the blossoms would float across the yard like snow, which we had never really seen. Across the street, there was an empty lot with fields of wild grass and trees. We built a tree fort over there and my kitty, Freddy, would follow us over sometimes. He would even see us off at the bus stop when we went to school each morning. I loved that cat!

The Greeks were not big animal lovers and we always had a menagerie of puppies or kittens for which we were trying to find homes. Sadly, we would find suffocated animals in bags that had been thrown in a large water drainage ditch near our home.

On many weekends, we would get away to the beach. It was our haven. Life was already grand but we all loved driving over the curvy mountain and getting to the shore. It was a cherished time as a family. Our drive would take us past acres and acres of olive trees with pale leaves floating in the breeze. Many traveling gypsies could be seen making their travels along the side of the road with their donkeys and carts. Always, before we reached the crystal clear ocean, there would be rows and rows of tall, wondrous Cyprus trees; they stood like tall statues even when the wind blew.

We would spend all day or weekend at the beach. I always found the sea to be so enchanting, the way the sun glistened upon the waves as they swayed inward to the shore. The water hypnotized me. Sometimes I would just walk along the soft sand looking for shells or pretty stones. I still have many of them. There would always be people kicking a soccer ball around, even in their bare feet. It didn't matter. We frequently would play soccer during recess at school.

On the yacht in the Aegean Sea with Dad, Mom, and Carol.

Snorkeling and diving for shells.

Mom would play with us in the water, or Dad would teach us how to play paddle ball. Dad used to call me his "Peanut" because I was so brown from the sun. I was the only one. Everyone else would burn first. I was this brown thing with white hair; everyone said it glowed in the dark. Funny, when I was little, I liked being different. Somehow it turned into such a curse later.

One summer we chartered a yacht. We went with two other families who were good friends. A good portion of the summer was spent on that wondrous boat. We sailed from island to island, and lived the most enchanting life for those weeks. Some days we would just jump off the boat and snorkel all day. I loved diving to the bottom looking for treasures. Other days we would pull up to islands and explore all day. There would be other boats in the port. Some were visitors, others were local fishermen. Always there were cafes, shops and restaurants that we eagerly visited after we tied up the boat. Wonderful, ambrosial smells of grilled meat, fresh fish and herbs wafted from kitchens, enticing our palates. My sisters and I loved to visit the markets and bargain with the shop owners. We could always get them to bring the price down on whatever it was we were buying. Dad taught us how to haggle a bit.

Mom and Dad would let us wander through the pure, white alleyways touched with geraniums and dainty flowers planted in pottery. Clothes blew in the wind, hanging over banisters or from clotheslines. The call of seagulls resonated.

The water truly was turquoise blue and we could see all the way down no matter how deep. We had a small boat that we could row to the tiny islands and picnic on. It was a joyful time. The men would catch octopus and hang them from the boat to eat later. All the kids thought they looked gross.

The sun beamed down on us adoringly. Everybody was colored from the rays, happy, and carefree. At night, we would fall asleep to the sound of waves splashing against the side of the boat. We would literally be rocked into dreamland, into tranquility.

Those years were so truly magical.

When we left Greece in 1973, the political atmosphere was tense. Our second stay there had been during the time of the US/ Soviet Cold War. Considering its geographical location, Greece was a hotbed for terrorist organizations. It was utilized as a link between Western Europe and the Middle East. There was violence targeted at Americans, as well as others throughout Europe. Within the year of our departing from Europe, there were three attacks against Americans: A bombing in Frankfurt (May 11, 1972), terrorists gunning down passengers on a flight in Athens (August 5, 1973), and a hostage situation and bombing in Rome (December 17, 1973). I remember imagining the bodies of the people killed in the bombings. All that was left of them would have been their charred bones and flesh. I couldn't even fathom being a child or loved one and losing someone in such a way. The military regime that governed Greece most of the time we were there was increasingly unpopular. There were undertones of hostility as a child I was becoming aware of, though maybe more subconsciously than otherwise.

Exploring Delphi.

Not long after we left Greece, a colleague and friend of my father's, Dick Welch, was executed. He was gunned down in his driveway days before Christmas by a terrorist organization known as *November 17*. He had been with his family at a holiday party. We would get snippets of information of such events, but never talked about them until much later. At the time, we had no idea that there was a CIA connection. I certainly did not fully grasp the huge ramifications of all of this until I was much older. At times there would be a certain awareness of things not being right. Many years later, I discovered that my father had replaced Dick Welch in Cyprus when we were on assignment there in 1964.

When Dad did reveal to us his "real" career, I don't think I fully comprehended what he was telling us. It took me years to try and understand what he did for a living. I never could; there were always secrets. Dad had such a wonderful way of circling around the truth.

It seems there was a price we all paid for the fairy tale life we lived. I didn't have lasting friendships. My education definitely lacked. Religion seemed to get hung up to dry somewhere along the line. My parent's relationship suffered. Self-esteem became a delicate issue during adolescence. Any confidence that I had was quickly lost.

FIVE

M y friends, rather the people that I was hanging out with in
Potomac, were not what you would call upright citizens or
high-achieving individuals. Some were high-school dropouts. Others
had been in jail and prided themselves on that fact. A lot of them
were cat burglars, people who quietly broke into houses while the
residents were still inside. Apparently, there was a real art to stealing
without getting caught.

I was getting quite an education from these people on how to
get money for drugs and booze. This became a hungry habit indeed.
I would take money from my parents. Sometimes we would go to
the mall or hangout on a street corner and panhandle money from
people. We would say that we were hungry and needed to get some
food, or were trying to get a bus back to our home in another town.
A lot of people were kind and gave us money. I didn't want to steal.
Nonetheless, it started to become a necessity to feed my habits.

During this drug-induced time, there was one evening when my
father was angry with me. Of course, I'm sure I was speaking to him
in a sassy way. He was unwavering in the stance that he took with me
that night. Dad slapped me hard in the face, leaving a red handprint
on my cheek. Each finger was easily distinguished. Dad had never
done this to any of us and this pierced my inner being more than the
sting on my skin.

I knew he was upset. I loved my father and mother. I never
meant to hurt them. But I was so lost and confused inside; they could
not reach me, no matter how they tried. Eventually, they could only
get my attention by doing something so out of the ordinary—like

slapping me in the face. More moments like these would occur with my father as he desperately tried to pull me back from the emotional abyss that I was approaching.

I found refuge in many different places - friends' houses, cars, the woods, and abandoned homes. I even slept in a church for a few nights.

Christine was my mainstay for a while. She could easily sneak me in because her mom was either smashed or passed out. Christine's dad was hardly ever around; he worked with the US News and World Report, always traveling around the world. Whenever he was at home, he was a charming man.

Christine had an abrasive personality, was a bit tomboyish, and definitely did not fit in. She also didn't give a shit. That was one thing I liked about her, that she didn't care what other people thought. Seeing how she grew up, I could understand. Christine's brother Lee had already done a few stints in jail and seemed quite proud of the little criminal record that he was developing. He had also left some nice decorations in the family home - numerous holes in the wall that he had punched out of rage.

Lee had introduced me to a biker gang that I stayed with for a few weeks. One of the ways they made money was by making methamphetamine and selling it. We stayed in an abandoned house next to the Village in the wintertime and it was like being in an igloo. There was one other girl there with them; she was a girlfriend. I thought she had the coolest clothes and boots. One of the guys—I'll call him Ray - I slept with every night to stay warm. We could see our breath when we would talk to each other; it was that cold. He never bothered me or tried to fondle me in any way.

We got blasted every night, and they threw parties. It seemed they knew a lot of people from the area. It appeared they were on the run and didn't stay in one place for long.

One day, Lee, Tom, Christine, and I were over at her house having mixed drinks from her parents' liquor cabinet, since they weren't at home. We all got smashed. The doorbell rang, and

Christine answered it. There were two undercover policemen, and they were looking for me. I tried to sneak around the back, but they saw me and grabbed me. I was handcuffed and taken to the police station. I had been called in as a "missing person."

I was supposed to go in front of a judge, but my parents did not want to go to court.

Instead they reported to me that, "We were going to see a doctor."

It was nothing new. I had been taken to see a lot of doctors. Why should this be any different?

I was in the back seat of our Volkswagen Bug and couldn't get out if I wanted to, though I had thought of trying to do so. There had been numerous times when the police had picked me up and I had gotten away. One time I was handcuffed to a bench at the police station, and I slipped my hand through the cuff. No problem. I guess that being thin and bony helped. When I got outside, I hitched a ride, and a Mack truck picked me up. I could always get a ride when I stuck my thumb out. As I rode down the street, the truck passed Mom and Dad on their way to the police station. They looked so distressed.

Now, it was me with mom and dad driving into the city—Washington, D.C.—in complete silence. Riding in the back of the Bug always made me nauseous because that's where the engine was. I felt like puking throughout the forty-five-minute drive, but I didn't want to talk to my parents.

We eventually arrived at a large complex of buildings, George Washington University Hospital. I really didn't suspect a thing. I thought we were just going to meet with a doctor. The shrink would ask me questions, and I would do my usual silent act, and then would leave. Without any words being spoken, the car was parked, and we entered the medical facility. My father told me to "wait over there," and pointed to some couches and chairs to the side of a large reception desk. Mom stayed by me.

I still didn't feel as if this would be anything other than another futile attempt to get me to open up to the latest in a lengthening line of shrinks. After approximately twenty-five minutes, my father joined us, without speaking. Frankly, my parents and I didn't know how to communicate. There was either silence or arguing. Things had descended so rapidly with my fall into addiction and warped behavior that they were desperate. So, we waited quietly for our "appointment." A hospital staff member then escorted us to the elevator and we went up.

Dr. Rosenberg was waiting for us at his office and in we went. It was not a joyous occasion.

They discussed how things had been going at home and school. They explained how out of control I had been for my parents, and the difficulty they had handling me. They were concerned about my drug and alcohol use, and the types of people I was interacting with. The stress I was causing was affecting my entire family.

I listened. How was I to respond? It was my journey. My road. My decisions. My life. Screw them.

Dr. Rosenberg and my parents discussed some therapy that I could receive at his facility. He said that the family could be included. And during this delightful one-hour session, I was informed that I would be staying there for thirty days.

Oh really? I was a bit miffed, but I suppose I should have seen it coming. As this was a decision my parents had already made, they went and retrieved my clothes and toiletries from the car. There was a brief good bye, and I wouldn't see them again until visiting day that weekend, and then for "family therapy."

It was 1976. I was fifteen and I was in an adult psychiatric ward.

SIX

Sleep did not come easily that night. I was irritable, sweaty and nauseous. In retrospect I realized I had withdrawal symptoms. Voices and moans emanated from nearby rooms, and the staff checked on us regularly. I suppose they needed to make sure that no one harmed himself or herself.

I woke the next morning to a bland breakfast. Certain people required special diets so meals were cooked to accommodate everyone. We all congregated in the dining room. Mealtime seemed to be a real delight to some of the patients. One of them sat down with me.

"How ya doin', Angel?" he asked.

"Lousy," I replied.

"My name is Eddie; let me know if you need anything."

"Thanks."

"What ya here for?"

"My parents put me here. I kept running away from home."

"Why?"

"Don't know."

"No problem, I'll leave you alone if you want me to."

"Thanks Eddie. I just don't like it here."

After breakfast, we had free time for half an hour. Some people went to their rooms; others went to the lobby to smoke or watch TV. We were allowed to make phone calls from the ward phones, if we had certain people on our "list." I only had my family on my list. I didn't feel much like talking to them, and I was sure they didn't want to talk to me. What I really wanted was to smoke a joint or drink a beer.

That day I had individual therapy, which had come to bore me by now. Mom and Dad had sent me to so many doctors in their attempt to find out what was "wrong" with me that meeting a shrink, any shrink, was tedious. I had nothing to say to these doctors. Most of them seemed pretty wacky themselves.

It was Dr. Rosenberg again. He started by asking me how it was going at the hospital.

"Fine," I replied.

"Have you talked to your parents yet?"

"No."

"Would you like to call them?"

"No."

"Do you know why you're here?"

I didn't answer.

"Patricia, do you realize that your parents are worried about you?"

Silence.

"Is there anything going on at home that you would like to discuss?"

Silence.

For an hour, there were just questions and silence. It was painful for both of us.

All of my "individual" sessions were like this, marked by silence. What was there to say? Dr. Rosenberg was not someone I really wanted to talk to; he was cold and unfriendly. I felt like I was under a microscope. In my mind, what he wanted was information to "report back" to my parents. To me, my feelings were private and difficult to explain. I certainly didn't want them to be analyzed.

Maybe it would have helped for me to give Dr. Rosenberg a little bit of history. Maybe I should have told him about a terrible fight between my mother and father that I had heard one night. It was when we were living in Rockville, about a year prior to the start of my rebellion. I was sharing a bedroom with Carol in the basement and it was late in the evening. I'm sure my parents thought we were sleeping, and my sisters were, so I was the only one who heard. My parents were obviously not happy with each other that evening. I could clearly hear Mom saying to Dad, "I don't want you! I can't take it anymore!"

This fight opened a new compartment in my mind. It showed me that there was something wrong between Mom and Dad. Though I never spoke of this episode to my sisters or my parents, it definitely affected me, and keeping it inside was probably not healthy.

I don't know why I didn't ask my parents about the disagreement, or just say something. But back then it seemed difficult to speak up about anything. So I carried it deep within my heart, and it became burdensome.

Privacy ruled our home and Mom and Dad displayed little affection toward one another in general. This didn't seem odd to me in any way because it's how I was brought up. As far as I knew, it was the norm. My father always seemed so "unavailable" emotionally and physically. Mom would have a hard time dealing with my sisters and me, so there was a lot of spanking and yelling. If we said naughty words, she would clean our mouths out with soap.

All my friends thought Mom and Dad were the cool parents, the neat parents. Everything always seemed fine between them. In our house, the mood was usually calm and low-key. Maybe it was too low-key. But when Mom got really upset with us kids, there was upheaval and anger.

And so I became what the psychiatrist called "the family scapegoat." I was the one that everybody focused on as the troublemaker, and then resented. I was the reason that Mom and Dad had to stay together. All families have dysfunction, but our family didn't deal with it. Instead, they focused on how screwed up I had become.

I suppose it might also have helped, in my sessions with Dr. Rosenberg and the other shrinks, to mention how I had felt when Dad had told me and my sisters one day, when I was about 14 years old, that he really didn't work for the United States Army but instead for the Central Intelligence Agency. Oh my God, what does that mean? That was all I could think of when he told us. It was just too overwhelming to handle. I think my first feeling was of betrayal.

When our family grew up in Greece and Cyprus, we spent a lot of time on the Army base or at the American Embassy. "CIA" had never been in our vocabulary. Dad would be gone for long periods of time now and then, but it was part of his job as far as we were concerned.

Around age 14 at the beginning of my decline into drugs and alcohol.

After Dad told us, he showed us pictures he had taken of us in Athens using his briefcase camera. I guess they were "test" shots for new equipment he had been issued. The photos were of my sisters and me walking through the city, unaware that the valise he carried had another use. Then he showed us a shoe phone, just like the kind we'd always seen Don Adams use on the television show, *Get Smart*.

So, Dad had been a spy. We were intrigued, but a bit baffled at the same time. I didn't fully understand what he did and it took a long time before I did.

From then on, when people asked me what my father did for a living and I told them, they would say, "Oh, he's a spook!" Well what did that imply? I had never heard that term. But then I started hearing it a lot. It seemed to insinuate something negative, but I adored my father and had the utmost respect for him. After a while, I didn't like to hear that kind of reaction, so I stopped telling people where my father worked.

My father had a job to do and secrecy went along with it. I could not comprehend all of this at the time but we were all expected to accept it nonetheless. Nothing was ever explained. Perhaps that would have helped. Growing up amongst secrecy and uncertainty was not the most wholesome nurturing environment.

Though my father loved us very much, his job was extremely important to him, and work always appeared to be the first priority. His job did provide us with a stimulating upbringing, and exposure to different cultures that I wouldn't have traded for anything. As my father would drag us through the museums in Greece, Rome, London and other European locales, and we would belly ache, he would always say, "Patricia, one day you will appreciate all this." And he was so right. As bad as things got later, I always said that I would never barter my childhood for anything, and I still wouldn't. I had lived a magical life before it crumbled.

And maybe I should have told Dr. Rosenberg what a nightmare it was moving to Potomac.

I was angry. I had no friends or relatives. All of our cousins, uncles, and aunts were strangers. We barely knew them growing up, so becoming acquainted with them as a young teenager was uncomfortable. My sisters and I were so rattled from being pulled away from Greece that it was all we could do to stay sane. My parents didn't know what to do.

I do know that when we moved from Greece to the United States, my parents had long discussions about what was best for us. They felt that our going to the States was a good decision and I don't blame them for it.

Like many towns or communities, Potomac had a way about it, though we were unaware of this initially.

Potomac was a place where the nouveau riche lived. They liked to flaunt their wealth with such things as big houses (what they call McMansions now), fancy cars, expensive clothes, pedicured toenails and fingernails, draping jewels, nannies, maids, gardeners, trips to the Caribbean—the list goes on and on. Before long, we were exposed to their kids and immersed in this moneyed environment.

Ironically, we did have a maid for most of our time overseas and for a short period we even had a gardener. Our maid had been more like an extension of the family, we adored her and she was not treated like a servant. We did not have extravagant clothes or showy cars.

I remember when we pulled in to our new Potomac neighborhood with the moving truck, on Thanksgiving Day, and our dog needed to run out and relieve herself, right on someone's lawn. The first words we heard from that neighbor was, "Could you please come and clean up the dog shit?"

Most of the other people around were about as friendly. We didn't hear "welcome to the neighborhood" from anyone except one family, the Silversteins. They were just the nicest people, one of the saving graces we had in Potomac. Mr. Silverstein worked at Northrop, the aerospace company, and Mrs. Silverstein stayed home and took care of their three children.

I suppose the timing of our move from Greece could not have been worse. I was at the bud of my adolescence; dealing with hormones and my body changing. It seemed to me that the chaos was too much to deal with emotionally.

In George Washington University Hospital, I thought about all this as Dr. Rosenberg asked questions and I didn't answer. He kept asking, over and over, "Why are you so angry, Patricia?" Where could I start? No one understood. My sisters and I never talked about the hardship of it all. We were all in survival mode when it came time to cope. Mom and Dad didn't converse with us about anything, and Dad was consumed with work. It all built up. Since I didn't really feel like telling some stranger sitting across the room from me with his notepad, I kept quiet. I felt I had no control over my life.

Was my situation and my agony really so dreadful that I needed to turn to drugs, skip school, run away from home and eventually end up on a psychiatric ward? The truth of the matter was, in my mind I could only find peace from my emotional angst in the drugs and booze. I hadn't gone off the deep end like some of the people I was surrounded by, but I was on a path to severe addiction. Once I took that first drink or smoked that first joint, it was all over for me; I had found my cure. This did not seem to enter Dr. Rosenberg's mind. I would not get help for alcohol and drug addiction until many years later.

Addiction is a mean warden that has no mercy and you are its prisoner. Your only crime is that one day long ago, you succumbed. I had waged a war that I would battle with myself and others. People who have never experienced this do not understand, and hopefully they never will. My wish is they can just take the word of an addict.

My spirit was slowly being robbed. I was suffocating it with substances. The innocent, rambunctious, blonde-haired girl that grew up on the Mediterranean was now engulfed in drugs and booze.

SEVEN

Free time on the psychiatric unit was okay. I got pretty good at ping-pong. Carly, the woman with the flattened-down hair, would come in, prance around, and entertain us all. She provided my comic relief. Sometimes we would both dance on the ping-pong table together. Or if we were having a bad day, we would tear things up or light fires in the bathroom. Her punishment would be shots of Thorazine. Because I was so young, I would get the "isolation room" with just a mattress—no sheets, so I wouldn't hang myself. And I would get what they called "match restriction." "Big shit," I thought.

Late one night, I was awakened by loud screaming that sounded like a sick bird screeching. I opened my eyes and was amazed to see an old woman in a wheelchair rolling herself into my room, crying. "My husband is dead, there is no one left, and I'm all alone. Please let me sleep in here," she sobbed, completely hysterical. And then, when I became more alert and sat up on my bed, I noticed that both of her legs were missing from the knees down.

Her name was Helga. A German with a heavy accent, she looked like she was in her eighties and had short white hair. Her face was wrinkled and scrunched. Life had obviously been hard and painful for her.

It seemed that she was all alone, and I'm not sure how long she had been on the ward. That night and for many nights later, I would stay up and talk to her, and so I learned her story. It seemed to comfort her that someone was willing to listen to her talk about her early life in Germany, when she was young, beautiful and married to a good husband. And I learned why she used a wheelchair; she had lost her legs to cancer and hadn't chosen prosthetics. Instead, knobs stuck out from her chair.

Helga mostly visited my room late at night, deflecting my mind from my own circumstances. Usually she came in with tears or the screaming, but I could calm her down. Occasionally, she needed to be sedated with meds, but it seemed that the staff was okay with her late-night escapades, since they never removed her from my room. She often fell asleep in her wheelchair. In a strange way, she made me feel better about my situation. My problems were temporary; hers were permanent.

One day, while we were playing ping-pong, Eddie, who had befriended me when I came in, started a conversation about his family.

"I have a daughter and a son," he said.

"Do you see them much?" I asked.

"No, they gave up on me years ago because of my drinking."

"I'm sorry, Eddie."

"It's my own fault."

"Stop drinking."

"I've tried."

"And?"

"I can't go longer than a few months."

"What happens?"

"The urge is too strong, and all my friends drink. It's like I can't live without it. Sometimes I don't want to. When I drink, it helps me deal with the pain of all that I've lost."

"Eddie, it's never too late."

"For me it is."

I knew how Eddie felt. I wanted to get high and drink. It wasn't an option for me at that time. But rage was. I had an attitude all the time, with the doctors, my parents, the other patients, objects that got in my way, and people that were supposedly helping me.

I found Eddie to be real hardcore. He was a Marine who had been in Vietnam. He wouldn't talk about Vietnam though, except to say that it was a place of "horror." He reminded me of a greaser type from the movies of the '50s. His hair was slicked back, and he had an edgy face. You could sense the war in his deep creases and troubled eyes. His frame was withered. He smoked a lot. I don't think his teeth were real; I didn't ask about them but I could just imagine him losing them in a bar fight.

As odd a pair as we may have seemed, Eddie was almost like a father to me during my stay, or maybe an uncle. We would sit by the window of the hospital lobby and talk on and on. He had voluntarily signed himself into the ward, so that he could come and go on passes as he wished. I, on the other hand, couldn't get out of there for the life of me. Even the elevator and windows were locked!

Eddie would go on passes for hours, and it was always a mystery to me where he went. I think any kind of female companionship was a comfort to him, even if he had to pay for it. And when I look back it, I have the feeling that's where some of his visits were spent. But I noticed that when he came in from his trips outside, he never smelled like booze. To my sheer delight, he always brought me back Chinese egg rolls with duck sauce, and they were one of the small pleasures during my stay at the psychiatric hospital. Eddie was merely being kind. He wanted nothing in return.

My contacts to the world outside were limited. During the family therapy sessions, my sisters would come in and scowl at me, while my parents would recount the events that led up to my hospitalization—after we had moved to Potomac, I got involved with the wrong crowd, started doing drugs and drinking, stopped going to school, started running away from home, and began to get into a lot of trouble.

It was quite obvious that my sisters were upset and annoyed with me. I had caused a lot of disruption in the family. Meanwhile, they were having difficulty dealing with their transitions. We had all become strangers. We had all been so close growing up, and now there were no words to be said between us. As I sat there during our therapy sessions, I was sure things would never be the same—ever.

A visit from my Uncle Jerry provided a nice break from my usual routine. He gave me a pep talk and hung out for a bit. Jerry was my mother's half brother. My mom's father had died when she was a baby and her mother remarried several years later. The two of them had four more children.

My Grandma Hoehn was overweight and suffered from multiple health issues. She was a dear woman, but always seemed worried and uptight. Her hair was always curled at the beauty parlor and she wore little makeup but dark lipstick on her thin lips. She loved it when we all came over for the holidays. There was always a huge table of food and loads of presents under the Christmas tree. All the furniture was covered in plastic so that it wouldn't get stained.

Grandpa Hoehn was also overweight. He had a big, round head and was balding. A devout Catholic, he liked to rattle on about his plant collection and religion. He also made me extremely uncomfortable. On several occasions, while over at the Hoehn house, Grandpa would announce that he was going upstairs to take a nap. He would ask me to come and wake him up in a short while. Once, when I went upstairs, his bedroom being at the top, there he was, lying completely naked on top of the sheets. He looked up and I ran downstairs. After that, I never felt obliged to go wake him again.

When we would stay at the Hoehns' for days or weekends during transitional periods, I loved doing things with my aunts and uncles. I didn't know them well, but they always made attempts to take us out for treats or show us the sights. It meant a lot. They lived in Washington, just over the line from Maryland, and would take me and my sisters to little donut shops or department stores with drive-in parking lots, a whole new concept to me. The drive-in garages always smelled like McDonald's French fries. We all loved going to McDonald's; there weren't any in Greece.

⊞

Not long after Jerry's visit, I met a new patient. His name was Walter, and he was an older gentleman. Well, I didn't exactly meet him; I just saw him sitting in a wheelchair in the lobby. Micky, who was always in the lobby smoking, had likely attempted to converse with him and had no luck. Walter would just sit there quietly. He was probably in his late seventies. Part of his face was bandaged. One of the other patients told me that Walter attempted suicide by shooting himself in the mouth, unsuccessfully. He had what seemed to be a bullet hole through one of his cheeks. His daughter would visit him and they would sit together in silence. It was awkward and sad. Who knows what was going through Walter's mind as he stared at the walls and ceiling trying to avoid his daughter's eye contact.

As the end of my stay on the ward slowly approached, I was able to take a few visits off grounds with staff. To my surprise, I didn't really have the urge to run. I didn't know why; maybe it was because I didn't know the city well. I had also been off the drugs and booze for a few weeks, so there was no longer a desperate need to get drunk or high. So, it was enjoyable to get out into the fresh air for an hour or so, even if it was with a bunch of crazy people from a psych ward who were supervised by the staff.

We walked a few blocks and then sat on some benches near some fragrant flowers. I smelled them, and almost appreciated their beauty. My mind had become so blank that I couldn't get in touch with my senses. But the flowers evoked memories of how when I was little, I loved running through the fields of poppies. They had no scent, but there were so many, it was like floating in crimson silk. My sisters and I would put them in our hair, and Mom relished the flowers that I plucked for her. We were amongst some of the oldest ruins in the world, outside Athens. Recalling these fond memories, my grief for the loss of my home expanded.

Going home from the hospital was dreadful. It felt as though my sisters hated me. My parents wanted me to be better. My behavior was monitored and I hated school more than ever. But I still returned to my friends, the booze, and drugs. I was already enraged, and was turning it up a notch. It was like being in a psych ward had been a rite of passage into the world of rebellion.

I spent 30 days in that crazy place and the doctors gave me no diagnosis; I was "defined" as having a dual personality. Mom and Dad were scared and helpless. Nobody had answers and I came out in worse shape. My addictions were still empowering. My fury was intensified. I was going to do what I wanted to do. I was right back out there, impulsively seeking the place where I was before.

EIGHT

adored my father, and I suspect that some of my angst stemmed from the need for more of his attention and approval when he was around. There would be blocks of time when he was gone for work. Our relationship was complicated, at least in my eyes. I'm not quite sure Dad knew what to do with four daughters. He grew up as an only child, raised by a single mother from the age of twelve.

I didn't understand my father very well. However, I indirectly found a way to resolve this dilemma. When I had borrowed money from my grandma Earnest, I would go to her house every month to pay it back. We would have dinner together and chat. It helped me bond with a woman with whom I had felt friction for many years. But it also allowed me to gain a new understanding of my father.

My Dad did not talk of personal matters much. He never talked about his father, whom I knew from his mother had died of a brain tumor. Not until I was a grown woman would I discover a few more details about how his father passed away, after inquiring.

Dad said, "They were bringing my father home from Johns Hopkins to see if anything could be done. The verdict was no."

"I don't know what they told my mother at the hospital."

"My father was put on a gurney and into the ambulance."

His dad, Edwin Burchett Earnest, who was 42 years old at the time, died on the way home; my father was with him. He was twelve years old.

After her husband died, Grandma Earnest took in boarders for a few years.

"Some people from the British Embassy stayed at our house, and we became good friends," Dad recalled.

Dad's mom then rented out their house after his father died. Dad recalled living in an apartment building across from the Cathedral in Washington, D.C. It was called the Alto Towers apartment building on Wisconsin Avenue which is still there. Dad stated that, "[My] father lived there with his parents when they first came to Washington for my grandfather to accept a position with the State Department."

"I would roller skate up and down Wisconsin Avenue as a boy," he remembered with a smile.

My father was always so good with detail and dates. He also recalled living in that apartment during World War II. They would not return to their original home until after my father graduated from Georgetown University.

Mom and Dad hiking the Sumerian Gorge during a family trip in Crete.

When I think about my grandmother, I remember a tiny, soft spoken, extremely strong willed Brit. I admire her resourcefulness and perseverance to accomplish what she did as a single mother in a foreign land. At one point, she helped with the cleaning at a boarding house in Iowa City when my grandfather was in Law School to make a living. I can't imagine how difficult it was for her, but by the time my father went off to college, she had earned her citizenship. She would also go to work for the State Department.

Grandma Earnest had worked hard to send Dad to prep school, so that he could then go off to college. All of her money went in to her son's care and advancement, who later described himself as a "dayhop;" he largely commuted to school rather than board.

"I would ride my bicycle to school if my mother needed to be away for her work," my father recalled. As a result of his mother often being away, as a boy my father would be allowed to board at Georgetown Prep for periods of time.

Dad graduated from Georgetown Prep School in 1951 and went on to study History and Government at Georgetown University, with a minor in philosophy.

My mother and father met at Georgetown University Drycleaners. They both worked there. My father took out front and my mom was a typist in the back office. He was a junior in college; she a junior in high school and only sixteen. She was living in a row house on 11th street in Northeast Washington, D.C., at the time. She would take the trolley to Holy Trinity High School, which she described as, "the worst Catholic girls' school at the time." Mom said she was a "tomboy" when she was younger. When I look at pictures from her youth, or even as a mother to us, she was gorgeous. My father was the very debonair type; they made a striking couple together.

My father was in the U.S. Marine Corps Platoon Leaders Class (PLC) while in college and was shipped off to Japan as a Marine after graduating. He and my mother were first engaged while they were both in school. My mother was offered a job with the FBI and

CIA because she was such a good typist. She worked at the Office of Security, CIA, in temporary office quarters that were set up along the Potomac River during World War II. While my father was away, my mother sent him an application from the Agency. When dad returned from Japan, my parents were married in June 1957.

Dad first worked for Woodward and Lothrop in the garden department, selling cameras, outdoor equipment, and sports gear. He then met with a CIA recruiter and joined the Agency in September 1957.

My mother had lost her father as well. He died from tuberculosis and diabetes when she was four months old. He had been placed in a sanitarium for people with contagious diseases, called The Glenn Dale. This was originally a reputable place for ill people to get quality medical attention. But then it fell to pieces and the building later became a mental institution. It looked ominous and was used in at least one horror film.

Her mother remarried four years later in 1943 to Frank. They met when they both worked for the government. Grace Butler became Grace Hoehn. Her husband immediately went off to the war (WWII) after being drafted by the Navy. Mom and her mother spent two years in Washington, D.C., but then went to Providence, Rhode Island, with her Aunt May to care for their sickly grandparents.

"My mother's grandma and Grandpa Butler lived there and they were strict," she said. "Lots of chores needed to be done."

During the war, my mother was allotted special food stamps for children that allowed her to get meat, which was a big deal at the time; everyone in the family would then get small portions of the meat.

When the war was over and Frank came home, mom and her parents lived in Virginia. She described this as a "grim" time. Mom said she had won a puppy at the fair and Grandma Hoehn tied it to the clothes line outside; she didn't like the puppy jumping on her legs. But one day mom came home and the puppy was gone. Grandma Hoehn had, "taken it to the black part of town."

By the time Mom was eleven years old, she had moved nine times! Grandma and Grandpa Hoehn also had four children, my mother's half sisters and brothers who she helped care for: Jimmy, Martha, Deidre and Jerry. According to my mother, Grandma Hoehn also suffered from migraines and anxiety; she was always sick.

Frank had difficulty finding work right away. Grandma Hoehn, on the other hand, "would spend money, accumulate debt, and then sell the house to pay off the debt." Mom stated that there were strange reasons for some of the moves as well, such as, "Grandma Hoehn always wanting to be near her sister, Aunt Irene. Or one house had termites so we had to move instead of treating them, because it would have been too costly. Another house had a tree that had branches that would brush up against the windows and this scared Grandma Hoehn. Mom said, "I couldn't keep up in school because we moved so much."

Everyone would go to the Catholic Youth Organization dances. I think my parents were both extremely smitten with each other and fell madly in love. It astounds me how young they were when they were married in 1957; my mother was only 19 years old for God's sake! My older sister Nancy was born here in the U.S. while they were still living in Glover Park. They then moved to Greece on my father's first assignment as a CIA Clandestine Service operations officer. He had been trained by now and spoke Modern Greek.

Mom and Dad moved to Athens in 1958 where we were until 1964.

My other two sisters and I were born in Greece. I was third in birth order.

Dad was stationed in Nicosia, Cyprus, from 1964 to 1966. When he first went, there was inter-communal fighting between the Greek Cypriots and the Turkish Cypriots.

When Dad first went to Cyprus, as a family we were separated from him for almost six months due to the fighting and hostility on the island. When we were able to rejoin him, we would go through checkpoints to get from the Turkish side to the Greek side.

There was a three-year period, a break between assignments, where we came home for two years and lived in Bethesda, 1966. We went back to Athens in 1969 until 1974; that was when we made our final return to the U.S.

Mom recalled Dad needing to drive in to work late at night to deal with cables that would come in to the Agency and had to be addressed immediately.

"Oh yes, that would have been part of the job at the time," my dad acknowledged.

I knew that Dad had turned down an assignment in the 1970's.

He recalled, "It would have been too much to drag you all around another country at the time." He also remembers passing up on assignments in Paris and Warsaw.

In 1978, my father was head of a task force involving the defection of a high-ranking Soviet diplomat, Arkady N. Shevchenko, an Under-Secretary of the UN, the highest ranking Soviet defector during the Cold War. Shevchenko served as a covert CIA source in his last years at the UN. I remember this job. There were glimpses into the world of how demanding and stressful it must have been for my father to head up such an undertaking. Dad and the Agency had this individual in a safe house for a period of time.

According to Mom and Dad, they decided to tell us about Dad's CIA career once we were in the US. Neither Dad nor I recall the exact details, but my recollection is that we were living in Potomac.

NINE

Something about Christine's brother, Lee, charmed the local girls, or at least Potomac's young, naïve, drug-using female population, which is where I fit in. One night, a whole pack of us partied in a hotel room. As the night wore on, most of the people started trickling out after drinking and drugging. I had felt ecstatic early in the evening, but everything had become blurry. The few of us that remained in the hotel room talked about sleeping arrangements, and it was decided that I would sleep with Lee, who had been touching me as the hours chipped away.

As we got under the sheets, Lee tore at my clothes and I allowed him to pull everything off. No, I was not flattered. Rather, as embarrassing as it sounds, I was confused about what he was doing. His eyes blankly looked into mine; both of us were past being intoxicated. He ran his hands across my body and fondled my breasts, roughly. He kissed me obtrusively and said nothing. He put his tongue in my mouth and ran it around my neck. He didn't know whether I found this pleasurable or not. Neither did I. He shoved himself in to me and I whimpered once or twice, barely moving. I mostly lay there silently; unaware of the huge loss I was experiencing or what a precious gift I was giving away. No emotions were attached to the loss of my virginity. If anything, our physical interaction sickened me with loss.

One or two days later, I felt discomfort in my crotch area. Finally, after almost a week, I went to a clinic and discovered that I had gotten crabs from Lee. It was humiliating and degrading. My innocence was gone. I had no pride, nor did I understand the concept of possessing any. I was 15, Lee was 20. I had no knowledge of statutory rape and I'm not sure what my parents would have done if they had found out. They knew little of where I was or what I was doing.

I met a young man named Tom during a day in the Village when I was 15. For lack of better judgment, I became enamored with him. He was handsome, with broad shoulders and a wide mouth of white teeth. Tom was 18 or 19 at the time, and initially he treated me well. I didn't realize it then, but he was a high school dropout. It seems what was important to me was that we liked to get high and drink together. Tom became possessive and abusive toward me. He was the first boyfriend who would speak to me in a demeaning way. Then he started hurting me physically. It was subtle at the beginning. Because I was usually high, I just couldn't think clearly enough about how I should have been dealt with as a young woman. I suppose because I felt the lack of emotional comfort from my father, I craved it from Tom. I saw his possessiveness and jealousy as love. He would fight to keep others away. How endearing, I would think.

One memory is of us going to a party and getting quite inebriated. I think because I was approached by other guys or talking to them, Tom became upset and slammed me around. I vividly remember him throwing me up against cars that were parked at the party. I begged him to stop. He then called my parents and told them I had gotten too drunk, and they needed to come and pick me up.

Tom tried to control me in part because I didn't care about myself. I thought his controlling ways were "love." Usually, I didn't have much say in what we did or where we went. If I did speak up, he would do things like grab my jaw so hard I thought he would break it. He would choke me and pull my hair. I know I was scared of him, but whenever we argued I would forget about my fear and attempt to fight him off. He would then come back at me with a force. My tiny body compared to his would get flung against walls by his big hands and arms. For a time, I would plead with him to not hurt me, it never helped.

The emotional mistreatment was scarring as well. He would make fun of how I looked or what I would wear. If I would ever talk about future aspirations (which was rare), he would stomp them down, declaring that I would never amount to anything. He was so belittling that my perception of myself became warped. I didn't talk to my family about my problems with Tom though, because despite putting up a tough wall on the outside, I was like a wounded animal inside.

There were countless times when Tom and I fought over the phone or face-to-face. Sometimes, if he didn't like what I said or how I acted, he would drive the car extremely fast and scare me. He would pretend that he was going to crash into trees or brick walls. Occasionally, he would leave me in the middle of nowhere. There was one horrible battle that we got into while we were driving. It was late at night and we were out in the country. Tom dumped me out in the middle of nowhere. I was in a panic. He came back about an hour later for me as I waited by the side of the road.

Whenever I went out with friends or without Tom, he would sit outside my house and wait for me. One night, he was drunk when he was parked outside my house. When I went out to talk to him, he began to sob after I got in the car.

"There's something you need to see," he said.

I was leaning with my elbow on my window when he reached into his right eye socket and pulled out an "eye." It was artificial. He laid it on the carpet in between the two seats. I couldn't look. But he kept yelling.

"Look, I only have one eye," he exclaimed. "My father was cutting the grass when I was little and a rock flew out into my face and I lost it." How horrible, I thought. Apparently this caused him a lot of problems from then on with school and self esteem. All the time we'd been dating, I hadn't the slightest idea that Tom had an artificial eye.

But maybe I should have sensed some issues. Tom had told me he'd actually been a semi-pro motocross racer, and that he was good. But I never saw him race. He may have lost his ability to ride along with his eye, but I'm just guessing. He probably needed a lot of confidence for the sport, and he seemed to lack that. He would still ride for fun in his back woods, but he could never compete. He also hated his father with a vengeance, but I don't know if that was just because of the accident.

Tom had a luscious race car that he would let me drive sometimes. Going 120 mph in a 1972 Roadrunner was an incredible rush! There were a lot of drag races on the weekends, in addition to the drinking and drugging. The smell of burning rubber became oh so sweet to me. And the sight of cars rolling out from clouds of smoke was a wondrous display. Speeding in those cars took me to another place; it was like a high in itself. It reminded me of how I felt as an airplane sped down the tarmac, just before lifting off. The crowd that we hung out with seemed to think that tricked out race cars and custom-painted 4x4 trucks were the ultimate indulgence. And they were all a bit older than me, so that made me feel as though I was part of a select group. I didn't mind that most of them were high-school-dropout losers.

Tom and I broke up and got back together as often as the sun came up. It was a bumpy, volatile relationship. When I would run away from home, he would sneak me into his house, and I would stay there without his parents really caring. They seemed intimidated by him. It was an odd family. They reminded me of hillbillies. His mom yelled a lot. His father seemed to get no respect and wore thick glasses that made his eyes look twice their size. Both of his parents chain-smoked, but Tom's dad also chewed on the filter. It was grotesque! They were from West Virginia, but lived in Maryland and held government jobs like many people around us did.

Sometimes I would sleep in Tom's car, either alone or with him. We would park in the middle of nowhere or behind a gas station. He and I would get in the back seat or just fall asleep in the front seats. Tom liked to have sex whether I wanted to or not. I didn't quite understand the whole concept as I hadn't been educated and the night with Lee hadn't taught me much, but I knew it was a physical part of a relationship. I knew how to perform and seemed to get better at it as time went on, but I didn't much enjoy it; the passion and desire just didn't seem to be there. Much to my dismay, the fact that Tom didn't care about my feelings, was hugely disappointing.

When I would run away from home, sleeping out in the car in the wintertime was absurd. I hated the cold. Tom would turn on the car and let the heat warm us for a while and then turn the engine off. When we would doze off with the engine off, it was unbearable. But we would have our booze and drugs, which helped. And the music helped. I would play Pink Floyd. Usually, I would listen to "Comfortably Numb" or the whole "Wish You Were Here" tape while I half froze to death in that car. What memories.

Christine remained a constant for me throughout my early relationships, sometimes sneaking me into her house. One time, we could hear her mom coming upstairs, so I ducked under her bed. Her mom came into her room and started talking to her while I was under the bed. It was actually humorous. Her mom was often inebriated; even though her rule was no drinking until 5:00 p.m. Christine's mom was speaking to her in a sweet tone of voice. By contrast, Christine always had a tough way about her, so it was interesting to hear this dialogue. I could tell Christine was trying to get rid of her mom, but it wasn't working so well. Several times, I ended up sleeping there, under the bed, all night. That's the first time I realized that I might have been a bit claustrophobic.

Christine and I spent many days at the exclusive Congressional Country Club, where her family was members. Even after I left the hospital, we would often get high somewhere, usually on the roof of a building. Then we would go to the dining room and get a delightful meal, the check for which Christine would sign with her parents' account number. She also would buy packs of cigarettes at the main desk in the same way. She always got some for me too.

We were easily bored amidst our luxurious surroundings, and frequently sought to "spice" things up a bit, especially when we were high. One day, we walked out to the golf course, where the PGA Tour regularly holds prestigious tournaments. The golf carts looked so tempting that we couldn't resist. So, we drove one around the gorgeous expanse like it was our playground, until a manager chased us down and made us surrender the cart. Suffice it to say, we got into a lot of trouble.

On occasion, Christine and I would do "normal" things together too. I went to my first concert with her. We saw Elton John. I loved watching him play that piano! He was amazing! Months after that, we saw Pink Floyd. They were one of my favorite bands. Of course, we were always high. Almost everybody in the stadium was high or drunk.

As a teenage runaway chasing my high, I was progressively getting into a lot of trouble. I had mastered the art of shoplifting. I would lift things like jewelry and clothes. Back then, before there were scanners and plastic security attachments, there was nothing difficult about tearing off a tag, putting a garment or a bracelet on, and walking out of the store with it. I suppose it was just a matter of having the guts or stupidity to pull this off. But my friends and I wanted things like cigarettes, and the stores were getting wise and putting them in cases where they were not so accessible for people like us. So we would ask the manager for a carton, walk around the store with it, and pull out a few packs. But this only worked a few times.

One day, I lifted a purse out of a woman's shopping cart in the grocery store. We got booze and drugs with the cash. It was probably a few six packs of beer (Budweiser at the time was about $1.60 for a six pack) and at least a $10.00 bag of pot. The credit cards were handy for awhile. Back then, they weren't as easy to trace. We could use them at gas stations or at the store for food or booze.

Tom loved the stolen credit cards, because his car went through a lot of gas. He would steal a license plate and put that on his car, because back then, the gas store attendants wrote down the tag number along with the credit card number. So every time he filled up his gas tank with one of the credit cards, he used a different tag number. It was smart and scandalous at the same time.

When I wasn't with Tom or a friend who had a car, I did a lot of hitchhiking. I always got a ride. Either I was alone or with a friend or two. Teenagers, mothers, fathers, truck drivers, anybody would pick us up—it didn't matter. We never gave a second thought to the possibility of danger. Never.

⊞

I was on the run all the time. My parents would call the police on me, but they couldn't arrest me for anything since I hadn't been caught doing anything illegal yet. My parents could call the authorities and report me as a "missing person," but that didn't seem to be enough to be pulled in to the court system.

All the local cops knew me, especially Officer Burke. He would always find me in Potomac Village with the "usuals." There could sometimes be 15 to 30 trucks, hot rods and motorcycles in the parking lot. But Burke never had anything on me. He loved harassing me, though. "What are you doing here? Where are you supposed to be?

Have you been drinking?" It became a routine. I was a familiar face to him, as he was to me.

By now, I had basically skipped class daily at Churchill High School and was eventually expelled due to lack of attendance. Here I was, throwing my life away. I had no future. It wasn't that I couldn't do anything. I had taken private piano lessons for seven years and even played in recitals. I had gotten an education in private schools across the globe. But I was wasting the talent I had. My life was going down the tubes rapidly, and I didn't care one bit. I was so out of touch with reality. I was an addict and an alcoholic. The truth of the matter was, I was losing my moral fabric, as I cultivated grim habits and warped thinking.

Occasionally, I would try to get some structure in my life. For a while, I had a job at a sandwich and ice cream shop. I helped behind the counter making sandwiches or ringing up the register. Somehow, I managed to hold this job for several months.

I thought I was so cool because the "older, tougher" crowd accepted me. The guys were always hitting on me. Here I was, 15 years old, and they were 19 and 20. The nickname "Angel" still stuck with me. Maybe it was my blonde hair or that I still had a shred of innocence left in me, though not much. Lee, my one-night stand who had quite a reputation, would always stand close to me and stare at me. He would play with my hair and stare at my body. He would tell me how beautiful I looked. These were compliments from a man; it made me feel a certain way that I enjoyed.

In a way, this crowd looked out for me. They always made sure I had drugs, booze, food, and a place to stay. They seemed protective of me, in a demented way. I felt wanted and accepted. Nobody laughed at me or called me names. Most of them carried buck knives and had been in fights on the streets and in jail. I felt safe. They shielded me from harm.

We had a joyous time in our world. Part of the thrill was being on the back of a Harley, speeding down the road in a race car, or romping through the muddy woods in a four wheel drive with everyone else who did not care. Happily, we would go to the Potomac River and party. There were hangouts where we would go to get away from the cops. All we wanted to do was party. No one had any plans for the future. It was never even discussed.

The truth of the matter was, I was directionless, and I could not see how I was destroying my life. I was fixated on drugs, booze, and detrimental relationships, which were now swallowing me, up alive. The only relationships that mattered to me were the ones that benefited my harmful habits. It didn't matter my plight or what price I paid. I valued nothing of myself.

I had gone so far astray that I was like a stranger to my parents and sisters. My substance abuse and acting out had irreparably damaged me and my family.

TEN

One weekend, I was out with Marie and Billy. Marie had been kicked out of her home for forging some of her father's checks, and she and Billy had said they were leaving town. I wanted to go with them. We had been doing a lot of partying and hanging out in Potomac, and decided we would sleep in a hotel that night.

I had some of my money from my paycheck. In fact, I had planned to go by the ice cream shop to pick up my last paycheck. They'd fired me because of my attitude. Part of my curt tone was due to a fight I had with Tom. He was angry about my wanting to leave town. We broke up.

Marie, Billy, and I stayed in a hotel for a few days. They had money left from the forged checks. We had parties every night. When we started running out of money, we decided to stay at Daphne's house; she was a friend of Marie's and her parents were out of town. Daphne's boyfriend, Phil, was a real bastard, and he didn't like the idea of us coming to stay there, but he couldn't do a thing about it. Billy and I would go to the store and rip off food for all of us.

Late, one evening, Phil came in with two runaway girls from Florida. He was roaring drunk. He was picking fights with everyone and demanded that we leave the house. Marie replied to him, "This isn't your house, asshole." Phil hit Marie in the face. I thought Billy was going to kill him. They both started fighting. They fell over furniture as pictures and glass broke. Phil pulled out a knife. Billy flashed his Buck knife, but Marie begged him, "Stop!" All the girls were screaming. It turned into sheer chaos. I panicked. Daphne hollered,

"You all need to get the hell out of here!" Marie pulled at Billy, and we scurried out.

It was late at night and close to freezing outside. There were few places for us to go at that time of the night. So, we hitched a ride to the Village and cooped up in the bathroom at the Amoco gas station. There was nowhere to lie down, nor did we want to. We drank what little we had with us and got stoned. When morning came, we headed to the high school, Churchill, where we ran into a friend of Marie's, Kerry. She had a car and was going home. When she asked us if we wanted to come, there were no questions asked.

At Kerry's, we sat around drinking beer, talking, and listening to music. Kerry had to go get her haircut, so she dropped us off in the Village. Billy said he had to get some clothes at his house, which was nearby. While Marie and I waited, she told me that Billy was going to break into Kerry's house. He had unlocked the basement door when we were over there earlier. I didn't have anywhere else to go, so I stayed with them.

We worried when Billy was gone for a long time. Marie and I got a friend to drive us down towards Kerry's house, but didn't say what was going on. When we got to Kerry's house, Billy was running out with a huge brown bag. We got back to Potomac and called a taxi. We drove to a hotel in Bethesda. In the bag were bills, change, and valuable coins. I couldn't believe Billy stole all of those possessions from Kerry's house.

I remember being deluged with emotions, but I "went along" with Billy and Marie. I didn't think about the possible legal ramifications of our brazen actions. Rather, they seemed exciting, and provided money for booze and drugs. Billy looked in the yellow pages to see what coin dealers were in the area, and there were several. He wanted to unload the merchandise quickly. He was nervous, but entranced with the possibilities of selling the coins. We got booze. Then I picked up my last paycheck. My mom had left a note for me at work. In it she wrote that she didn't understand what was happening to me, and ended, "I love you."

We called lots of friends and said we were having a party. Word spread quickly. Maybe 15-20 people showed up. I think half of them stayed because they were too drunk to drive. There was an abundance of liquor and drugs.

The next day, as people slithered out, Billy, Marie, and I slowly prepared for the day and contemplated our plans. We thought it might be better to get out of town, perhaps to go to the beach. There was a knock on the door. I went to answer without hesitation and looked through the peephole. COPS! Oh My God! It slowly sank in. They were calling out, "Police, open up!"

The rest of it felt like a movie in slow motion. I opened the door, and it was slammed against me. I was immediately grabbed and thrust against the wall. We were told that we were suspects in a "breaking and entering" that had occurred and that they were going to search the room. We were all held with our arms up against the wall and frisked.

It literally felt as if a human shredder tore the room apart. Mattresses were pulled off the bed. Furniture was moved. Purses were dumped. Lamps were undone. Toilet bowls were inspected. As much trouble as I'd been in, I didn't know a room could legally be messed up so thoroughly. They found a lot of contraband that way.

The stolen coins were found, or what was left. Billy had sold most of them for what was a rather large sum of money at the time, though I can't remember exactly how much now. Drugs were found, mostly weed and some speed. A lot of booze was there, which was legal for Marie and Billy to have, but not for me since I was a juvenile. I also had some stolen credit cards on me along with drug paraphernalia. We were each handcuffed individually and read our rights, then taken in separate cars to the Bethesda police station. I knew I was in a lot of trouble this time, and I was pretty nervous. But there was still a thought in the back of my head that I would get out of this somehow, or that I could run away. I still felt invincible.

Being processed at the station was an ordeal. I was interrogated, fingerprinted, photographed, questioned again, and treated like a criminal. I was handcuffed the whole time. Meanwhile, my parents had been called, but were told that I could not go home. I would be going to a shelter now because I faced criminal charges and would have to go before a judge. My parents did not come to the station.

Kerry did show up at the police station. The cops had her scan my jewelry to see if any of it had been stolen from her house. It wasn't. Then Kerry blasted me with venomous words. She didn't know that I really was not part of the "plan," but probably would have ripped me anyway. I suppose I could have gotten away from Billy and Marie when I found out about it, or I could have reported them. Admittedly, I was indirectly a culprit. Billy and Marie were the people I was hanging with at the time. They were the ones with the drugs and the booze. And when I found out there was going to be a hotel room to stay in, so much the better. I was not feeling contrite at the time.

Kerry had every right to be enraged with me. I only wish she had known the truth. And this had become an underlying theme for me so often. "If only" they had known the truth. My parents, my sisters, the kids at school, the teachers, and so on. All the people who I felt misunderstood me. But most of all, they couldn't see that I was now an addict and had no choice but to chase my drugs and feed my cravings.

I was driven in a van to a shelter. There were other juveniles that were being transported there or to other facilities. Everyone was handcuffed; some were cuffed to each other. The shelter was just a holding place for kids until they went to court or were sentenced to long-term facilities. It was a locked place in the middle of nowhere. I was hungry when we all got there but we had to be "processed" when we arrived. We were searched, questioned, given the rules, and assigned a room. There was protocol that had to be followed constantly. Regulations had to be kept. By now, it was late, and dinnertime had passed. We could get something from the kitchen if we could find something. They had these big milk machines.

The chocolate milk felt so good going down my throat. It was cold and creamy.

Since it was a Friday, I was to stay there for the weekend. The people seemed okay. I fit right in; I was young, angry, and in trouble with the law. But there is something about losing your freedom, as I had begun to find out in the psych ward at George Washington University Hospital. People tell you what to do and when to do it. You can't talk to your friends or see them. It's strange being locked in a room. I had no idea what it was like to lose my freedom until I really had lost it. I had turned from a wounded, injured animal into a wild creature that had been running and running.

Monday morning, I was picked up by the sheriff department's van. There were already four or five other delinquents, seemingly ages 14 to 18, in the van on their way to the courthouse. Everyone just gave a "knowing" look to the other; like, "yeah, we know where we're going."

We got to the courthouse and were all put into individual cells. It was like a cell from the old Western movies. A metal table and bench welded to the floor. And there was a metal toilet to relieve yourself in if you so desired; the guards kept an eye on you so there was no such thing as privacy. You couldn't see anyone else in their cells but knew that they were there. There were no metal bars per say, just a wall to enclose the cell and a door with a tiny window. The guards walked by regularly to check on us. Mainly, they wanted to be sure we didn't hurt ourselves.

There were many messages carved into the walls, bench, and floors. Grim thoughts like "kill me" or "the end is near." Or just something obnoxious like "fuck you." Some people just put their names. Others drew hearts with their names and their romantic interest's.

It was a dark place, figuratively and literally. But I wasn't fazed. It was par for the course that I was on at the time. My anger and the chip on my shoulder consumed me and carried me for a long time in that world. My fury helped me survive. I was a badass. The police and courts were just a slight inconvenience.

All I could think about was getting back out and using. "When can I get some booze and consume drugs? I have places to go," I thought.

I heard people in the other cells. Some of them were talking, moaning, or laughing. Some were silent. The muteness was almost like a sound of its own.

A lawyer, Mr. Topping, came to speak with me. My parents had hired him. He was tall with brown, wavy hair. He had friendly, blue eyes and a mustache. Mr. Topping was a genteel man. He smoked a pipe and was much like a character out of a movie.

He told me I was in deep trouble. I had quite a few charges against me, including accessory to breaking and entering, possession of stolen credit cards, possession of drug paraphernalia and possession of drugs—whoa! Also, because I was a minor, and Marie and Billy were adults, I was more at the mercy of the courts. They could be bonded out until a hearing, but I couldn't. I also had been out of control at home, and it was questionable whether my parents would even want me back. And, there was a good possibility that I would become a "ward of the state," which meant my parents couldn't take me home even if they wanted to.

When it was my turn to appear in front of the judge, the Montgomery County Sheriff's deputy came and handcuffed me. I was taken upstairs and into the courtroom. There I was, handcuffed, for my family to see. I remember being out of it and angry, but I know this image had a huge effect on my parents and sisters. I was assigned to Judge Tracy, who was a middle-aged, mild-mannered man. He was distinguished looking, with white hair. He was one of the three juvenile court judges in the county at the time. He took my case seriously and wanted me to do the same. He felt that my charges did not warrant my being able to go home. My parents were also apprehensive about my going home. I was made a ward of the state.

Mr. Topping, my lawyer, came to see me in the holding cell while I waited to appear before the judge. He told me about a place called Karma House that my parents wanted me to go to. He said it was like a group home and that I would have to be accepted in before I could go. Apparently it was a "tough" program, and I could end up being there for as long as a year, but I could earn freedom along the way. It sounded interesting. Mr. Topping said I needed to plead guilty for this to happen.

Soon, I went in front of the judge. My parents and my sisters saw me dragged out in handcuffs again. How degrading. I couldn't look at them, yet I felt no remorse. I was blinded by my belligerence and my addictions.

I was found guilty for possession of stolen goods, since when I was arrested I still had the credit cards on me from months before. And I was found guilty for being an accessory to breaking and entering, since I'd known what Billy had done. But Judge Tracy presented me with a "deal." If I would go to Karma House, probably for nine months to a year, to complete the program, then I would not face the 30 to 60 days in a detention center that he would give me otherwise. Instead, I would come out and be on probation, likely for a year or two. He was trying to mitigate my situation and, in his opinion, this was a fair solution.

"No," I said, "I'm not interested in going to Karma House." Everyone, including Judge Tracy, my parents, and the lawyer, seemed shocked and disappointed. But I said to myself, "I wasn't going to some dumb group home!"

Judge Tracy sent me to Flass Detention Center for 30 days, and told me I would return to court again.

"Okay," I thought, "I suppose I can deal with that." Home didn't seem to be an option anymore. Losing my freedom was tough to deal with, but I thought I could spare a month out of my life. There was no interaction between me and my family. We were like strangers. I know it tore at my parents' hearts, especially Mom's.

Immediately afterwards, I was handcuffed again and taken down to the holding cell. There I waited until the personnel from the Sheriff's Office came to get me and everyone else. Waiting is a hard thing, especially when you're not going to an unfamiliar and likely unpleasant place.

We did get lunch. We were all given paper bags that contained two pieces of bread with a slice of cheese in the middle. Our drink was a carton of what I later learned was referred to as "bug juice." I'm not sure why. Maybe it was because if it was thrown at bugs it would kill them because it tasted so bad! Yes, my journey as a convict was off to a nice start.

The detainees were all picked up at around five or six. I guess you lose track of time because it doesn't really matter anyway. It's not yours anymore.

"Be tough," was all I could think to myself. "You have no choice. You cannot show any signs of weakness; this is not the world for it." It was all too surreal.

I had the same people from the Sheriff's office driving me. They were actually kind to me. It was a small comfort. Everyone was handcuffed, some to each other. There were a lot of drop offs. The ones who were handcuffed to each other went in together. The various facilities consisted of shelters, detention centers, and boot camps. We eventually got to Flass Detention Center.

I was the only drop off for this place. In fact, I was the last drop off of the day. It was now quite late in the night. What a long day. We checked into the front desk with the guards. I was uncuffed, and the deputies left. The last familiar faces I had known were gone.

An unfriendly, big, stocky man read me the rules. They were as follows:

1. Follow staff directions
2. No fighting
3. No physical contact with staff or peers
4. No matches or cigarettes in possession except on breaks
5. No AWOL or discussion of AWOL

6. No food in rooms

7. No harm to selves

8. No drugs or paraphernalia

9. No sharp objects in rooms

He told me that there would be consequences for breaking the rules or committing any other inappropriate behavior. He said I would be searched. The female staff would search the girls and vise versa for the boys. I was checked EVERYWHERE. I would shower and be sprayed with a chemical that would ensure that I wouldn't bring anything in like crabs or lice.

We walked through a hallway lined with door after door. Big metal doors. Heavy doors. The type you couldn't get out of if you wanted to. Each one was unlocked and then locked as we went through. I thought of "Get Smart" and all those doors Don Adams would go through at the start of the show, booming and clanging behind him. Only this didn't feel like a TV show, but more like a horror movie. The opening, shutting, opening, and banging of the doors disturbed my psyche.

I was given green state clothes to wear for my stay. I was shown my "room." I was locked in for a night's sleep.

Sleep is but a word.

Everyone was awakened at 6:30 a.m. for breakfast. We were all lined up and marched downstairs to the dining hall where there was a foul stench; I felt nauseous from the smell. We lined up and grabbed a tray and plastic flatware. I looked at the food and it was all I could do to refrain from vomiting. I literally gagged at the sight and smell of the food. I didn't recognize any of what they were serving. Some of the other delinquents talked to me while we waited. Nobody seemed so bad… yet.

The food was absolutely disgusting. It was scrapple, which is made from parts of the pig that I don't think are edible, like the brains. There were the parts that they wouldn't even put in sausage or hot dogs. And then there was this watery sauce sloshed all over it;

probably to cover how horrible it really was. I couldn't bring myself to eat.

⌗

I had always been a finicky eater. Mom and Dad would make me sit at the table until everything was cleared from my plate. I could sit for a long time. They would catch on after a while when I would give the dog food under the table. That worked for a bit. Or I would try to swallow fish sticks down with milk. Even though I would gag and want to throw up, I could get the food down, which is what I was "supposed to do." Or, exercising my brand of humor, I would get up from the table and Mom would yell at me. She would chase me around the house like a screaming banshee. It was funny, so I would laugh. And then she couldn't help but laugh too.

When everyone else would order fancy meals at the swank hotels or restaurants in Europe, I would just want toast without butter. We would joke about that later. But the food in the detention center was no laughing matter.

I gained weight there from eating only starches. The bread and desserts were about all I could tolerate. I couldn't eat much there; it really was putrid. I would want to puke as I walked to the cafeteria. The smell couldn't be ignored.

Eating was important to a lot of the other kids. Fights were fought over food. There was little to look forward to; some people took pleasure in eating. It also broke up the monotony. My face started to break out too. I don't know if it was from the food or the stress. I looked pale. My eyes were sunken with no life, and my hair darkened from lack of sunshine.

The rooms that we slept in were down several hallways. Of course, the boys were separated from the girls. Everyone resided in his or her own room, which was tiny. It was locked at all times when you were in there, which was at bedtime or when you had earned "consequences," which could be often.

At night, the staff walked the hallways. You never got used to the sound of clinking keys. And you had to accept that they were going to shine that big flash light into your room, onto your face. Although they were checking on you for your safety and theirs, the lack of privacy felt intrusive. You didn't know what the male staffers were really looking at when you did sleep.

The nights were agonizing. You never got a restful sleep. There was always a feeling of uneasiness, unrest, and sorrow. Everyone was agitated. At night you would have nightmares. But when you woke up your reality was being in a true hellhole.

Occasionally, you would hear screaming, and you would see someone dragged out of his or her room and taken to some mysterious place. Or, you would hear people antagonize each other through the doorways and windows. Staff seemed to keep it under control. The staff members were husky. They seemed to lack compassion. That's not what they were there for. They were there to do a job.

The room, which was probably nine by nine feet, had a metal bed with a plastic mattress. If you weren't suicidal, you got sheets. There was also a plastic pillow on the mattress. There were metal bars on the window and a fluorescent light on the ceiling. That was it.

Yeah, I was a tough bitch.

Everyone loved getting mail; it was one of those small pleasures that meant a lot. I wrote to Tom and he wrote back to me saying he missed me. Marie also wrote me and wanted me to lie in court. No, I wasn't willing to do that for her; she had her freedom, and I was locked up.

A lot of the people at Flass Detention Center were from the inner city or from other counties, like Prince George's County. Most of them were African-American. Everyone, white or black, would give me the "look down." The boys would do a lot of posturing with each other. There was a ping-pong table and TV in the common room. There were always several groups of people playing cards, while the guards watched everything.

I didn't come from the world that most of the people there were from. I didn't look like I belonged. I knew they were thinking, "What in the fuck is this white, blonde bitch doing here?"

Cigarettes were divvied out over breaks, about five times a day. "God help me," I thought. With my habit, that wasn't many cigarettes at all. And your cigarettes came from whoever came to visit you and felt kind enough to bring you some.

A guy came up to me and said his name was Steve. He had long, shaggy blonde hair. He was from Montgomery County too. Steve was in for stealing cars and drug possession. We hung out for a while and then it was cigarette break time. I liked Steve.

I liked playing ping-pong. For the most part, I stayed out of trouble. Believe me, you weren't there to make friends. But you could make enemies quickly and mysteriously. If you looked at someone the wrong way, then you had to watch your back. Or if they thought you'd looked at them the wrong way, they wanted to jump you.

While at Flass, I received three days in my room for "talking AWOL." Someone must have heard me suggesting whether it was even conceivable to "run" or not and I got "narked on."

When you did time in your room, it meant you stayed in for 24 hours a day except to shower. They brought your meals to you. And they constantly monitored you through the little window on your door. God forbid you would try to hurt yourself.

I think by the third day I had cut up my arms and hands with the jagged edge of my plastic knife. I didn't do much damage. I'm sure I could have done much worse if I had really wanted to. I was bored.

My parents would come to visit me on Sundays, but it seemed that we would always argue. They came to see me on Easter and brought me candy, and that was a thoughtful treat. It was always a reprieve from the routine when Mom and Dad came. But I was in bad shape; I was grappling with withdrawal. Agitated, I sweated and shook. I couldn't sleep or eat, and I had diarrhea.

One day I had been off room restriction for a few days, and was mingling in the group area. There was this one great, big comfy chair that everybody liked to sit in by the TV. I had been sitting in it before cigarette call. When I came back after my cigarette, there was a big guy sitting in it. I told him he needed to get out. How stupid was that? He hit me so hard in the back of my head that I saw stars for about 20 minutes and was vomiting all night. I figured I deserved it for opening my big mouth. I actually got time in my room for that too, three days for fighting. Funny—I didn't remember doing any fighting.

Before getting clobbered in the back of the head due to my obvious lack of judgment, I had been undaunted by the whole institutionalized experience. I realized at that point that I could get seriously hurt. I wasn't sure if I really cared.

I had another run in with a girl that I thought was a friendly acquaintance. Her name was Shirley and she was from Prince George's County. We had all gone through the lunch line and gotten our mush for the afternoon feast.

Shirley asked, "Could I have your Jell-O?"

"Fuck no," I answered. "This is about one of the only things I'll eat around here."

Well, it was either the way I said it or because the answer was "no" that Shirley lunged across the table and swung at me. I saw her coming, so I avoided the first hit and aimed at her, but I missed too. We both ended up on the floor punching away, scratching, and pulling each other's hair. It didn't last long because the staff broke it up quickly. After that, I knew I could at least hold my own if I had to. I got three days for fighting. I'll admit I was fighting that time. I never got my Jell-O.

Here I was the daughter that everyone called the "black sheep of the family." I was always the different one. It had been so humorous, in a way, and I could use it to my advantage. I reveled in being unique. But it wasn't funny anymore. Now a dark cloud hung over me. Out of my three sisters and me, I was the only one who gravitated to drugs and booze. Why me?

ELEVEN

I did my 30 days at Flass Detention Center and was back on my way to the courthouse with my friends, the Sheriff's deputies, on April 13, 1977. In an odd way, despite their needing to handcuff me and take me to these destinations, they were hospitable about it. Obviously, these men knew my plight. It was always the same two deputies. I didn't know their names, but they knew mine. They would try and talk to me. Sometimes, they would let me sit in the seat that was furthest away from the other detainees and not have to be handcuffed to another person.

That day, it was back to the cell to await my appearance in front of Judge Tracy. I knew I was trying his patience. He told me I could go to Karma House if I felt like I could make a commitment there, or go to Montrose Detention Center until there was a bed available at Shepherd Place.

"Okay," I said, "I'll try Karma House."

In order to go to Karma House, I would first need to be accepted. And if I were not successful there, I would be sent to Montrose for three months to at least a year. The interview at Karma House was grueling. There were four counselors in the room, and me. I was questioned: Why did I want to come to Karma House? What kind of commitment was I going to make to the program and my family, as far as changing my ways and taking responsibility for my behavior? Did I understand how the rules worked and that at the beginning I would be followed around by a staff or peer until I could be trusted? Was it clear to me that I would have to contribute to the household chores and do my part as a member?

The counselors told me that as time went on, they would determine how I was progressing. They seemed hesitant to take me. My attitude was definitely an issue. But I think they took great pity on my mother and father and how desperate they both were.

I was going down the tubes quick. I knew that Karma House was not a locked facility and that there was the potential for me to run if I couldn't take it. There were options. But I didn't like the idea of time hanging over my head. I was accepted.

In the meantime I was released to the custody of my parents. We went to a restaurant on Shady Grove Road, which was down the street from Karma House. We didn't have much to say to each other. They were delighted to see me eat a good meal and I swallowed it down whole. I probably looked like a wild animal at the table. I think they were excited about my going to Karma. But I really didn't feel inclined to go, because I knew I might be there for a long time.

Karma House was an actual home just north of Rockville. It was close to my stomping grounds. There were only seven other girls there, and they all had various issues. Most of them were serious about getting out of Karma House the right way.

Life at Karma House was structured. The counselors lived there 24/7. We would all make our meals, clean up, participate in school and group meetings, do extracurricular activities, and have some down time. The whole idea was that we were kept busy.

There was a boys' Karma House too. But it wasn't close by. At times we would see them for social events, but we were watched closely so there was no physical contact.

While I was new, I had to have someone with me at all times. The rule was I had to ask someone to supervise me, staff or peer, and it was up to them to give me their time. It was annoying, but humbling, and that was the whole idea. I understood the concept; it was to gain trust and be more responsible in the house. You had to really want to get to that point. But they didn't make it easy.

I was at Karma House during the summertime. I remember sitting out on the porch and watching the cars go by on Shady Grove

Road. I would think about Tom in his Roadrunner. I wondered if he was thinking about me too.

My friend at Karma House was Sylvia. She was from DC. Sylvia had been there a brief time. She got there before me, which was long enough to get tired of it. It was not our time to commit to any program; we might have been too jaded at that point.

I think what did me in was a trip to Great Falls, not far away, by the Potomac River. We were able to go there as a group. Of course when you are somewhere being escorted by a bunch of counselors and all the other girls are trying to go straight, it's completely different than when you've been down to the same place with your friends getting drunk and high.

While I was at Great Falls with the girls from Karma House, I kept looking for everyone or their cars. I didn't know what I would do if I saw someone I knew—run or hide. It was excruciating. I wasn't ready to lose my freedom like this and work to regain it.

Sylvia and I spoke that evening and came up with a plan. I was still on "supervision" so we would sneak out the bathroom window while we ran the water to mask the noise. We knew that the police would be called and be looking for us, since we were both at Karma House under court order.

We got out pretty easily the next night. At first, we didn't know which direction to run. Both of us were nervous and excited at the same time. If we went right to the main road the cops would see us. There was a field we ran through for about 10 minutes and then took a chance on Route 28. When we hitched a ride we got picked up right away and got a ride to Interstate 270. We decided to go downtown and stay with some friends of hers that night. I remember the car on the Beltway, exiting to Crystal City, in Virginia. This was not my territory, but it didn't matter.

Sylvia knew her way around. I remember going to a big, old stone house, where a friend of hers lived. The trees were huge and the neighborhood reminded me of the kind you see in horror flicks. It was a cool, old area. I liked it. We got so high. I felt like I had come home and I could stay there for a long time. All was well. What was our big plan for the future? We would go to Potomac! Of course Tom would be thrilled to see me and my friends could find places for us to stay and it would be a big party.

We got on the road the next day and hitched to Potomac. It took a few hours. We got to Potomac Village, and soon after we arrived I saw Tom's car. We just looked at each other from afar. It was odd. He was hanging out with his best friend. There were other people in their cars too. Tom saw me. Sylvia and I were at the pay phone where I was calling Marie. She told me she and Billy had gotten out on bond, but Billy ended up in jail for something else. I told her that the police were after me and I didn't have anywhere to go. She said she would call me right back.

Meanwhile, Tom and his friend left. About ten minutes later the phone rang, and at the same time a police car pulled up. The officer knew who we were and told us to get in and we were taken to the Bethesda police station. I recognized one of the officers there from the bust at the hotel. They let me call my Mom, and I told her I was sorry for everything.

Two detectives came to pick us up. I was going back to Flass Detention Center, and Sylvia was going to a shelter home. I never saw her again.

❖

Months and months later, I found out that Tom had called the police on us. I felt betrayed by this person who told me he loved me. I wanted more time on the streets.

I went right back to Flass Detention Center from the station until I could be taken to court the next day. There were no more comfy shelters for me to go to where I could possibly run. I was in court the next day.

Again, the same two deputies picked me up.

It was back to the cell, and back in front of Judge Tracy. Suffice it to say, he was not happy. I knew he would be throwing the book at me and I was prepared. My sole regret at that moment was that I had only bought a minuscule amount of freedom. Sylvia and I never should have gone to Potomac when we ran from Karma House. My street smarts should have told me that the cops would go there looking for me, but I was turning into a burn out.

Judge Tracy was a serious man and he seemed distressed by my predicament. In his opinion, which was not an easy one, Montrose would be the best option at that point. I would return to his courtroom again in thirty days.

I had now been assigned a probation officer, Beverly Johnson. She was a youngish, somewhat odd black woman. She had a lisp and didn't come across as remotely warm.

Thus, I was off to Montrose.

TWELVE

My parents looked like I had just died when the ruling was made. They had remained hopeful that I would straighten out my attitude; they knew where I was now going. I could barely look at them for I was so detached from them at that point. It was humiliating for them to see me shackled in handcuffs.

They did not know what awaited me in Montrose, but to me it was just another facility. I could handle it, no problem. I would find, though, that I had no idea what type of despair lay ahead.

I waited in the musty cell the rest of the day until the deputies came. They were bewildered. "You again?" they asked. In a world gone so miserably wrong, these men seemed to care. As odd as it sounds, it meant a lot.

It was a long drive to Montrose. I had no idea where I was, but it turned out to be Reisterstown, Maryland, northwest of Baltimore. I'll never forget the name of that town. Even as a grown woman, when I saw signs for that town, my soul was rendered weak.

Judge Tracy had warned me he would send me here, though he had agonized over the decision. In the end, I had given him no choice. I was defiant, cocky, and stubborn. Montrose was the fourth facility I had been holed up in by then, not including the psychiatric ward that Mom and Dad sent me to the previous year.

Montrose sat on six hundred acres of large fields and bushy trees. It had been a plantation long ago, and I imagined it then, being beautiful and prosperous. Large, old trees hung as if sobbing. Fuzzy, dry, brown grass begged for a manicure. Little roads ran through the sprawling grounds. We would drive along them in rusty, old vehicles, kicking up pebbles and rocks. In the hot summer, dirt would blow in through the windows, making me cough.

Betsy Patterson, who resided in the mansion with her son, Jerome Bonaparte, originally owned the land. Because it was not far from Baltimore, many of the residents who were eventually placed there were Baltimoreans. The lush land then went through several owners before it was bought by the State of Maryland in the early 1900s. In 1922, Montrose became a juvenile facility for girls.

Originally, the campus was composed of the mansion and several cottages. Another campus with additional cottages was built to accommodate more students. Montrose was referred to as a "training school" for girls for nearly 50 years, until the early 70s, when the population became co-ed. The school's population consisted of minor court committed youth or more severe cases that warranted the need for incarceration.

Montrose had been created as a "last resort" for "hard core" offenders. However, more than 40 percent of its population had charges consistent with violation of probation and truancy. Less than thirty percent of the young offenders at the facility were charged with a violent crime.

Montrose became a "warehouse" so to speak, as there were few options for treatment at the time this facility existed. Unfortunately, a status quo developed in the type of population that became predominant at Montrose: Black, inner–city youths, many locked away inappropriately, but still out of sight from society. Almost at all times, each bed was filled.

It was dark when the deputies dropped me off to begin my stay. Two boys that were cuffed together were also dropped off. I was escorted into the deteriorating residential hall in which I would be staying. Each had a name and 15 to 20 people. I stayed in the Guttmacher Cottage.

The staff had cold demeanors and gave me the rundown of the rules. I was uncuffed, stripped and searched. Normally only the women could put their hands on the girls, but later I would find that this was not always the case. Almost all of those who worked at Montrose were intimidating figures. Their big, gruff hands searching me were intrusive and injurious. In my opinion, I was cooperative and didn't feel that the cruel introduction I received was warranted. I was given the horrid bug spray and told to shower. At that point, my belongings were limited. Anything that was of value (or possibly dangerous), would be taken and locked up to be returned upon release. I only had one outfit. They said they would get me some more clothes later. We were not assigned State regulation clothes at Montrose.

I was locked into my room for the night. It had a rotten stench, and paint peeled from every surface. The walls were an ugly plaster that had been painted a horrid, puke-colored yellow. They were pocked with holes and covered with stains, signatures, graffiti, and initials. One wall had a tiny, barred window from which you could view the boys' cottages and a massive magnolia tree. Ordinarily, this tree would have been a prize. But in such a distorted environment, it had lost all its beauty. The door to the room had a little window for the staff to look in and view us. Up until then I had thought I could handle anything. I was tough. But it was different here at Montrose, as I would soon find out. What in the hell was I doing here?

As I attempted to settle into my teeny, locked room and inspected it closely, I could see BLOOD on the walls. Red gore was splattered all over. It was as if someone had violently caused harm to herself and it splashed onto the wall. Some of it was smeared on the yellow plaster. I wanted to scream, bury my head and pretend it didn't exist. I felt like barfing.

"Please somebody get me out of here, I don't want to be here. Please, help me!"

Nobody could hear me. The wailing was in my head. It was always in my head.

Into the night, I wondered about the spatters. I felt like the room was going to start dripping blood onto me, and I longed for home. My brain was exploding.

The worst part about the red smudge on the walls was that I had to guess, I had to imagine why it was there. I didn't know. But "they" did. The staff knew the freakish smears were there. Were they trying to scare me? If they were, it was not working. I wasn't frightened yet, I was rattled. Actually, I was furious.

How could I put it out of my mind? There was no possible way that I could. It horrified me in a way that was personal. I had been witness to the anguish that someone else had felt in my room. The blood on my walls had a poignant effect on my psyche.

In the middle of the night, I went to use the bathroom. While I was in there, I was getting paper towels to clean the stains. The staff wanted to know what I was doing. I told them. They said it would have to wait until morning. No problem. ("Fuck you" I thought to myself).

As usual, I struggled to sleep on my plastic mattress, the kind whose cleanliness I had started to question after my numerous incarcerations and confinements. Sleep was a luxury from another time in those places. The staff looked in on me all night; I guess they worry about you when you first check in. And then there were the keys. The incessant jangling sound becomes disturbing to your ears. You never get used to that noise. Not only the clanking, but what it represents: The total loss of freedom.

They were trying to cripple my spirit.

***

All the girls were awakened at 6:00 a.m. to prepare for breakfast. Our doors were unlocked and I could hear people trickling out of their rooms. People sounded grumpy. One of the first greetings I got was: "We got us a new bitch."

We all used one large bathroom. The massive sink in the middle had a sprinkler-like faucet. The old, dirty toilets were all in stalls, like at a school. Cracks sprawled across the walls. Thank God there were at least individual showers with curtains. You could smell ammonia, but there was still mold on the curtains and in the corners of the showers. You never got used to going in there, nor would you want to.

I wasn't used to what other girls did in bathrooms, especially girls from other cultures. African American girls did a lot of different things with their hair. They would spend massive amounts of time in front of the mirror braiding, pressing, putting oil in. It was quite a process. And when you would have a conversation with these girls, they wouldn't talk to you; they would talk to themselves in the mirror. I almost envied their arrogance. They had come from abominable homes, but they didn't care to give me the time of day. Most of the girls were from Baltimore, a place where I had never been. They didn't care whether I acknowledged them or not. I was one of three white girls out of fifteen in my unit.

I grabbed some paper towels from the bathroom and took them to my room. One of the girls was laughing at me and thought I had an accident in my bed. I didn't care; I just wanted to clean my walls. It seems the blood had been there for quite a while, or it wasn't as easy a task to get off as I thought it would be. Going back to the bathroom a second time caused even more hysteria and ridicule, but I finally got my walls clean. It didn't mean I would rest well.

Soon after I got to Montrose, I discovered huge cockroaches. They were all over the place, including our bedrooms. Up until that point in my life I had never seen anything like them before. But the other girls and the staff seemed to be comfortable with these big, juicy bugs. I think bedtime was the worst time for all of us, for various reasons, like the bugs, nightmares, noise, and staff looking in on us.

I did not get a welcome party. Instead, it was made clear that I better watch my back. I was becoming familiar with the intimidation at these places. I knew I had to keep myself in check, "or else." It was the usual—don't give anybody the wrong look, blah, blah, blah. Or, I would get deluged with the ridiculous statement, "Girl, you better check yourself," if someone didn't like what you had done or said.

Kissing ass means giving other girls your cigarettes or doing what they want you to do. I wasn't willing to do that. If you bumped into someone by accident, then they would want you to "check yourself." And they would knock into you on purpose. I wasn't willing to play their game. They didn't like you confronting them in group meetings. My mouth always seemed to get me in trouble, and I hated seeing other people getting pushed around.

I suppose my "mouth" was my way of finally speaking up. I never said anything when all the kids in Potomac called me names and gave me venomous looks. I never said anything when I was torn from my beloved Greece. I never said anything when I was dragged to all the shrinks that Mom and Dad sent me to. I never said anything when Lee stole my virginity. I never said anything when Tom started abusing me and a lifetime of it began....

Girls would incite you by saying things about "your mama." This actually would enrage a lot of people. I know it would get me going sometimes. Or if you gave someone a scowl, this could often be reason enough to fight. Everyone was filled with fury or bordered on insanity. Most of the girls didn't want to be there, though from what I heard, a slight few of them did find it more comfortable than their home environment, which was sad. We were such a bitter, hopeless bunch.

One of the rules was that we had to participate in the cottage meetings that we had every day. Girls were constantly confronting each other about "issues" in the cottage. Many of the girls with strong personalities were good at creating chaos and stirring up trouble. The staff loved the dynamics that went on. It entertained them. Usually, there were would be provocation during meetings that would start fights. It was inevitable.

We all had chores that we had to do. The ladies in the kitchen were really sweet; they were the only friendly staff that worked there. I liked signing up for kitchen duty, because then I knew the other girls wouldn't mess with my food. If someone didn't like you, it was guaranteed your food would get spit on or they would blow snot on it. Sometimes I would go a day or two without eating, depending on which girls had been working in the kitchen. I only made a few friends at Montrose, but we tried to stick close to each other.

Simone was a tall, white girl with red hair and brown eyes. She used to be a prostitute and she seemed cool. Whenever anybody gave me a hard time, Simone would stick up for me.

Blanch was a pretty, African American girl about my size. She could never speak at a tone below a shout. We got along and that was all that mattered.

Tanya was an African American girl with slanted eyes. She didn't like a lot of people and called me her "buddy." Tanya would get into a lot of fights, which would constantly earn her at least twenty-four hours of isolation in her room.

Lisa was a skinny, white girl whom I had also known in Flass. She had brown, curly hair and blue eyes. Since she had arrived in Montrose, she had become quiet, but I would try and talk to her.

I'll never forget Tamar. She was from Dundalk, which is part of the inner city of Baltimore. Tamar was always yelling at you or someone else. She was relentless with her hollering. Her tone of voice would literally pierce your eardrums. She was a light skinned, African-American girl with wild hair that she would put in rollers at nighttime. She was scary. Tamar had a reputation for starting a lot of scraps and was famous for having "no mercy." She was strong and she was hard to ignore. The staff favored her, so she would take advantage and get away with a lot. Tamar was missing some of her front teeth. There were other people I had come across in Montrose and other centers that had missing teeth. How could this be? They were so young! Soon I would find out that it was from fighting or abuse. This was so foreign to me.

Most of the youth appeared to be there for minor offenses or merely running away from home. But a lot of people were there for drug possession, assault, theft, shoplifting, and so on. Rumor had it that there was a guy there for manslaughter. He had killed a store owner during a robbery. And supposedly there was also a girl there for murder. She had killed her mother, intentionally. I guess she was seventeen and would possibly be tried as an adult. The story was that her mom, who was a crack addict, would let men molest her daughter.

There were always fights. Up at the school there were gang bangs. The boys would push the girls into the bathrooms and have their way with them. I stayed out of the hallways and never used the bathrooms in the school. It was total anarchy in the school; almost anything went and the staff would allow it. The security staff would decide what went and what didn't, depending on who you were. I learned at that point in my life that some individuals who were in a position of authority could either use it in a good way ... or not.

It was the staff that was hardest to get along with, and they could make you or break you.

The staff had their favorites, and I wasn't one of them. I didn't like following rules or kissing ass. The staff could also give you "write-ups," which would go to court with you. Apparently, the write-ups would have an impact on how your case or future place-ment was determined, so staff would hold them over your head constantly. They also had their keys.

The staff would give us "consequences" if our behavior was bad but not severe enough to warrant isolation in our rooms. They would have us do things like sweep, mop, and buff the stairway with a rag. You had no choice but to do the last on your hands and knees. There were sixteen steps. Cleaning them in such a manner made them seem like a massive amount. If you were working while the girls had to go up or down, then you would get a little kick on the side from one of the people who didn't like you.

After being there a few weeks, a girl who was on "suicide watch" was locked in the room across the hall from me. Staff had to observe her twenty-four hours a day. She had tried to slash her wrist with a pair of scissors that she had swiped from their office. They were angry at her for going into their domain, but also for it happening on their time. They had no compassion for her.

I could hear her moan and cry all the time. The staff had taken all of her clothes. She was naked. I could see them taunting her. Eventually, they moved her up to the infirmary where she would get medical attention. Apparently, she was in bad shape and kept trying to hurt herself. I didn't know why she couldn't have been sent home, and I never learned what happened to her. I wondered about her quite a bit, however. At least, it helped take the focus off my misery.

I started writing home and begged them to get me out of Montrose. I wasn't sure how safe I would be. I would get into verbal or physical altercations and get locked in my room all the time. If I earned room time, the staff allowed the girls to ridicule me from outside my door's window. They would bang on the glass and yell into the room laughing and mocking me. There was a pecking order according to the staff's whimsy, and I was not a part of it.

My mom had heard rumors through friends back home that I had been sexually molested at the school in Montrose. This was upsetting to my mother. I was dealing with rumors. I was far away from home, in a living hell, and this is what people were saying about me? I was crushed. Who were my friends? What would I go home to when I got there?

In Montrose, it was difficult to hold on to your scruples; you questioned every little thing. This world I had entered was breaking me and I wondered about the inhumanity that I witnessed.

When you feel swallowed up in these places, there is a lot of thought put into the cement walls and huge, locked doors. I confess that I didn't reflect back on my severe misjudgments and deplorable behavior. Instead, the rage over everything lost had become the focus and raw emotions would well up and have nowhere to go. Even when I got out, my anger was quite apparent.

Mom and Dad came to visit one day. I was ecstatic to see them! The staff had me in isolation. When I walked downstairs from my locked room to see who my visitors were and saw them, I embraced them and couldn't let go. I hugged Dad tightly and he held onto me too. I wept uncontrollably; it seemed that there were a lot of cooped-up emotions. Being off the booze and drugs sent me into quite a state, I suppose. I probably could have used a lot of help for my addictions, but my drug and alcohol problem was never brought up or dealt with. Never. My heart was so delicate at that point in time.

As far and distant that I had grown from my parents, that one afternoon we became close like we never had before. It was like nothing had ever happened. It was like I wasn't locked in this grotesque place. It was almost as if I had gone for a visit somewhere and would be coming home soon.

Dad gave me his handkerchief to wipe my tears. When he and Mom left, I felt heartbroken. I was so alone and depressed. I didn't know how to deal with it. I slept with Dad's handkerchief under my pillow for days; it had the scent of his cologne on it, and somehow that gave me comfort.

My thirty days at Montrose were almost up. I would be going back to court to see what my long-term plan would be. Thinking that I wasn't coming back, I would mouth off and not follow directions. This didn't make life much easier on me with the staff and other girls, but I abhorred all of them. I hated life, I despised Potomac, I loathed what I had become, I hated that I didn't know how things had gotten so ugly, and there just didn't seem any way out. I had set a wicked course for myself, and I didn't know how to get out, how to get help.

As usual, the deputies came to pick me up. They were one small comfort in all the chaos. It was a long ride from Reisterstown, Maryland, to the Montgomery County Courthouse. Into the cell I went to await my destiny. One would think that you would get used to those cells. You didn't. They were cold and damp. They really didn't want you to be comfy there. Why should you be? You are a bad person, a criminal. You're there because you have done something wrong.

At this point, my heart was feeling empathetic towards Mom, Dad, and my sisters. I actually felt remorse for what I had put them through. I loved them so much and I knew it had been dismal for them. There was a plethora of emotions that I was feeling, but none that I could clearly sort through in my head and heart. I wanted them to let me come home. But I understood their ambivalence.

There was no turning back. I didn't even consciously think about the path I had taken. While I was in over my head, I had passed the point of no return. If only someone knew what I had been going through and had tried reaching me, then maybe I would have listened.

THIRTEEN

My fate was in the hands of Judge Tracy once again. I knew his heart was growing heavy with making the decisions over what to do with me. It was obvious to him that I needed to "dry out" but there were not many drug/alcohol facilities then and treatment was not widespread.

He told me I could go back to Karma House if I felt like I could commit, or go back to Montrose until there was a bed available at Shepherd Place. Of course, all of those stays would be approximately one year long! One year of my short life! I shuddered at the thought. There was no way around it, no running away, and no getting out of the handcuffs. I had to pay for my actions.

It was unlikely that the staff at Karma House would take me back, but I decided to try nonetheless. In my heart I knew I really didn't want to be there, but it was better than going to Montrose. I also didn't know much about Shepherd Place.

Mom and Dad drove me to the interview. There were about four or five counselors. The head honcho was there. Two of them had been there the momentous night Sylvia and I had run away. I did not want to face them. They asked me why I was there and why on earth I wanted to come back to Karma House. I tried half-heartedly telling them. The two staff members who were there when I ran away went into detail about how they remembered that night, and that they knew I was going to run. They knew I was not sincere then or now. They could see right through me. They said I took advantage of people and that I was a manipulator. They then proceeded to ream me out, and told me I would not be accepted back. Of course, that meant that I would be returning to Montrose.

I had to go back to Montrose. Oh God, please, no. I wanted to die.

There was only darkness now. I was in shell shock. There was no denying my reality.

How could I go back? It was so horrific! My brain throbbed. My hands trembled. My chest thumped. Gloom pulled at my heart. It was too much, too much.

My parents drove me to Montrose. It was a quiet, solemn drive. There were no words to be spoken. The professionals had told them that I couldn't be reached. One of the detectives at the police station had told Mom, "Your daughter is too far gone and you need to give up on her." My mother was outraged. She told the detective, "Don't you ever tell a mother that, I will NEVER give up hope for my daughter!"

The psychiatrist that visited me while I was in Flass Detention Center said that I had a split personality. I'm sure my sinister attitude and withdrawal over not having drugs and booze had a lot to do with my extreme moodiness.

Mom and Dad had been told by counselors, my probation officer, intake officers, the lawyer, and others that I was in such bad shape, I would never get better. My parents were told that this would probably be my life now—in and out of the courts and time in detention centers. I suppose I probably would have believed it at the time too. This did seem to be the direction that my life was heading in now.

Here I was, going back to Montrose after I had told everybody to "fuck off." It was not going to be pretty. I don't think I felt so apprehensive about anything in my life up until that point.

I was scared.

Oh, but I was welcomed back at Montrose. It was made clear that my ass was mud as soon as any opportunity arose.

I remember clearly one night being kept up by one big, black girl who was new. She was not able to sleep and was yelling out of her locked room. A lot of us were telling her to shut up because we were being kept awake. The next morning as we were walking down the stairs to breakfast, I sharply said to her, "You are one noisy bitch!" She charged at me and it was all I could do to brace myself. She pushed me down a few stairs first. I felt lucky for not falling. We both went at it. It was like we were punching away in fast motion. But she was too massive and strong. I did eventually go down. Then she started kicking me as hard as she could; first in the head, then in the stomach. The searing pain as her hard shoes went into me was more than I could bear. It felt as though bones were breaking and veins were popping. I faded in and out of consciousness. Staff must have gotten her off of me at some point, but I don't know how long it took them to pull her off.

Next thing I knew I was at the hospital. I had a couple of hairline fractures in my ribs, a concussion, and I had been spitting up and urinating blood. It felt like every inch of my body was broken. I felt like a split twig inside and out.

I just wanted to lie in bed and let someone take care of me, like when I was little and Mom would bring me noodles with butter. Or like when I was sick and she would mend me back to health while I listened to the Beatles on the record player.

Unfortunately, I was sent back to the Cottage that night. I wanted to wallow in my misery and pain. I think they kept me in the infirmary for a day or two during school time, which helped. Going to the Cottage felt awful as I was still reeling from the fight. People seemed willing to give me my space, which was appreciated, but there is never a time that you let up on watching your back. It's exhausting, especially when you're hurt and tired. I was injured and felt pathetic. But I didn't feel like I wanted to prove anything anymore. I was on the fringe; I was frail.

After that, I kept to myself. I kept my mouth shut. I just wanted to do my time and move on. Where I was going I didn't know, but it couldn't be any worse than where I was. I honestly felt like I was in hell.

One day, I got a visit from Beverly Johnson, my court-appointed probation officer. She meant well, and did seem to care, in her own way. Beverly informed me that I would be on probation for two years after I got out. At that point, I didn't know what that meant. She also told me that I was awaiting a spot at Shepherd Place, which was run by nuns and staff members. It would be a lot better than Montrose. It was semi-locked. If I ran, the police would be informed, and I would immediately be arrested. If that happened, I was back at square one. She said that I would probably be at Shepherd Place for about a year.

Well, I wasn't quite too sure what to do with all this information. It was a lot to digest. All I could think of was getting out of Montrose. And then I start thinking about being somewhere else for a year.

That was a lot of time. Hadn't my "time served" counted for anything? Time was meaningful to me. Somehow, I coveted this fleeting concept.

Beverly and I did talk about the time not necessarily being definitive. She said, "Patricia, if you do well, you can get out in less time. It's up to you." She also reminded me, "Patricia, you have not been a model citizen up until this point in the court's eyes. A lot of people don't hold much stock in you right now."

She said that even if the court released me, my parents were petrified of taking me home. They knew I would revert back to my old behavior. I had a long way to go. I had a lot to prove. And I had a lot of people to whom I had to demonstrate my commitment to change.

In the end, I spent a little more than sixty days at Montrose, and I will never, ever forget the place. Years later it was closed for being so inhumane—big surprise.

Montrose had whipped the hell out of me, yet somehow I had survived. I had plodded through without getting raped. I didn't lose any teeth. I didn't try to kill anybody or myself. I didn't kiss ass. In my eyes, I kept some of my "street" dignity. I hung onto myself as best I could. I was glad to be moving on. Any place after that would be like paradise.

Looking back now, I can see that Montrose became something I could use in a good way; it scared me. If nothing had shaken me up, then I would have kept going in the direction I was heading. I was already in the grips of addiction, for which I was not getting help. But I was also succumbing to a life of crime. I would have undoubtedly ended up on the streets as a prostitute or homeless. Even worse, I could have ended up dead. Yet, my heart needed to follow my mind. As an addict, I was torn.

Still, when I left Montrose, it was like leaving a piece of me behind. It had torn away at me like nothing has ever since. It was like a vulture flew down and took a bite out of me, but it kept pecking away. It has had a chunk of me my whole life. I didn't really talk about Montrose for almost 30 years. I could only write about it here, in this memoir. How can you possibly describe such a savage place? Even worse, how do you explain how you got there in the first place? People would think you were crazy.

I prayed to God that I would never have to go back to that living hell, but that was going to be up to me now. It seemed I was more breakable than I ever realized or would admit. It took me years to come to peace with my ordeal.

To my detriment, Montrose had changed me in a horrible, monstrous way. It made me build a shell to survive, a hard exterior. There was an ugly beast that grew in me at Montrose. I had seen things there. I had felt things there. I had feared things there that

I had survived. But I took the wounds, the scars. It took me a long time to soften from Montrose.

You don't just shake it out of your system. It becomes part of you.

I had so much shame when I was there, and no sense of self.

FOURTEEN

My parents were going to take me home for the weekend before I entered Shepherd Place. I knew they were scared.

It had been more than four months since I had been home. Sixty-three of those days had been in Montrose. That was a long time for a 15-year-old. I was becoming "institutionalized." Or to put it another way, I was "in juvie."

I would be on my best behavior at home. I was by no means ready to blow it, despite my desperate need to get high or drink. At that point, I was realizing what I had put my family through. I had been unkind, selfish, and mean spirited.

But my heart ached too, though no one wanted to hear how I was addicted. Drug reliance is difficult to understand. My world and the people around me weren't ready to take that on yet.

Going home was like going to another world. I felt alienated from my sisters. I didn't blame them. I think I called a few friends. I called Tom. It seemed we were still in some sort of weird, dysfunctional relationship. But I knew I shouldn't see him.

When I was in Flass Detention Center, Karma House and finally Montrose, I wrote Tom all the time. My wants were powerful—for him, home, drugs, booze, or anything to forget where I was. I think he wrote back twice. I lived for those letters. In one of them he sent a picture of his wrecked Roadrunner. He had been racing and it rolled over about three or four times. He was lucky to be alive. Funny, his letters were telling. They were about one and a half pages long. He couldn't spell. Tom never even graduated from high school, for God's sake!

I don't remember going out and doing a lot as a family. I'm sure Nancy, Carol and Sheila probably expressed a dislike for that idea. I was not allowed to get together with any friends. That was okay. I understood. I was glad to be home, to enjoy real food, and not worry about anybody coming after me. I don't remember sleeping well. It was just too foreign. As comfortable as it was, I couldn't get used to it. Maybe it was because I wasn't there to stay, and I really wasn't a welcome guest. That's what I was, a guest. It was kind of like, "okay, let's see how this goes, and if you're good, then we can try it again another time."

I knew I had gotten myself there. But even now, it's hard for me not to look back and remember what Dr. Rosenberg said about being the scapegoat.

The weekend passed quickly, as I knew it would. The trip to Shepherd Place had come. All I knew was that it had to be better than Montrose. I could deal with that, even if I had to be there for a long time. I would do my time.

Mom and Dad both took me. This all took a lot of time away from Sheila, Carol, and Nancy. No wonder they resented me. If only they knew, though. If only they knew.

The drive had been awkward, as usual. They both tried to offer words of encouragement. They told me Shepherd Place was a nice facility, and that there was a waiting list. They told me, again, that nuns ran it. That was interesting. It reminded me of the nuns that were at the Catholic schools we attended. Some of them seemed genuine, while others seemed quite crabby.

Even then, religion seemed bigger than life. I believed in God and He was a crucial part of my life. And I always felt angels around me. When I was tiny, I scooted over in my bed, against the wall so that my guardian angels would have room to lie down. There seemed great comfort in this then, and even though we had strayed from the Church, I was glad to have had the exposure to God, or a Higher Power, in whatever form He took now.

Age 16 at Shepherd Place.

We go to Shepherd Place and it certainly looked pleasant. As we drove up, there were tennis courts and beautiful grounds. We parked and walked to the admission desk. It took a little while. I don't remember being nervous, just anxious about where I was possibly going to spend the next year of my life.

After I was admitted at the front desk, Sister Catherine came to get me. She was the one running my unit. There were the usual formal greetings with my parents and me. My parents were polite. They almost seemed meek.

Sister reminded me of one of the nuns from my Catholic school days. She had her habit on, which was black, with her hair covered by her wimple, of course. Her face was pale. She had whiskers and wore glasses. You could see a bit of gray sticking out from her cloth fold. Sister Catherine was probably in her fifties, and had some wrinkles. Her bluish eyes looked blood shot.

My parents accompanied me to the unit and Sister Catherine went over the rules with us. We walked through long hallways where there were little classrooms and therapists' offices. There was a courtyard in the middle. It looked nice. But compared to where I'd been, anything would have seemed like heaven.

I had a room that was a step up from where I had been. I even had a closet! I had packed a suitcase of clothes, since I would be there a while. I didn't hang any pictures on the walls. I didn't bring any photographs of my family from home. I didn't really know what "home" meant at that point. I had blown it so badly with my parents and sisters that a lot would be foreign to me when I did finally go back. I didn't want to surround myself with anything that was an emotional reminder of what did not or may never exist—a renewed relationship with my family.

I had learned that it would be thirty to sixty days before I could "earn" a weekend home. According to the rules, if you were on good behavior, you would get certain privileges. So it all depended on me when I would get to go home again.

Meanwhile, I had to say my goodbyes to Mom and Dad. They looked sorrowful and tired. They looked different. I had done this to them, to Sheila, Nancy, and Carol. I was a bad person. I felt hollow.

There were five other girls on the unit, and seven units in addition to ours. Most of the girls were from Baltimore, though some were from Montgomery County, like me. After Montrose, that did not sound good. They were all in school when first I arrived at the unit. When they returned, we sat in the day room, where all the unit meetings would take place. There was an informal meeting with Sister Catherine, the other staff (who were not nuns, but young women), and the other girls. We all introduced ourselves to each other. There was a mixture of white girls and African-Americans. There was definitely a different feeling here than in the places where I had just come from. Everybody seemed pretty nice. We had "free time" before dinner.

Most of the girls liked to hang out in the "groom room." That's where they would all get ready before going home on weekends. Or they would just pretty themselves in there for whatever. I wouldn't be going home on a weekend for a while.

We would walk through multiple hallways to get to the cafeteria. There was the smell of food; it was not extremely pleasant. All the girls would go through and the line ladies would serve them their dinner. Some of the food was optional. And there were things like dessert selections. Wow, choices. I wasn't sure if I could handle it!

We would all sit at assigned tables, according to our units. But we had some freedom about which girls we wanted to sit with. Nice! Compared to where I had been, the food was not too bad. In a lot of the places, it had been hard to even identify some of what you were eating. Food did not become a comfort to me like it did to the other girls. I thought it was disgusting in these places.

When we returned to the unit, there was time to hang out and watch TV. We would then have a meeting. I suppose I was apprehensive about the meeting since it had been a sour point at Montrose. Usually there would be arguments and fights would break out.

That first meeting at Shepherd Place wasn't bad. A few girls talked to someone I'll call "Susan" about stealing. Apparently, she had been taking things from the girls' rooms. They all seemed to be handling it well, except for her. She denied stealing from anyone. The staff handled the meeting in such a way that they tried to get her to take responsibility for her actions. I guessed I was going to have to keep an eye on Susan.

We had a little bit of time before retiring for the evening. As usual, I tossed and turned. I don't think any of my nights in those places were restful. How could they possibly be?

We were awakened at 6:00 to get ready for school. Tired juvies are not pleasant in the morning, and may be more irritable than most grumps in the early hours of the day. The bathroom allowed some privacy. Separate stalls and showers. You become thankful for these things after you have been deprived of them. They come to really mean a lot.

I kept to myself.

After showers, we drifted down to breakfast. The smell made me want to barf. I really wasn't a breakfast person, and this kind of

113

food was not for me early in the morning. But girls were begging me to get food for them, so that wasn't a problem.

Everyone ate and we walked back up to the unit. The girls primped a bit more, and off to school we went. All the different locations went through mazes of hallways and ramps. It was actually a nice place. I was able to appreciate the fact that it felt cozy and clean compared to where I had been. The staff seemed respectful and fair to everyone. There were no boys to deal with, which I guess was a good thing because they had been a threat at certain times in Montrose.

The classrooms were set up by subject, not grade. They would figure out how far behind you were. Certainly, nobody was ahead in her academics. I had missed so much school. It's really hard to say how much of an education I got between junior high and high school. At Shepherd Place, they did the best they could to instill something in us.

Shepherd Place 1977.

On Sundays, when most of the girls were gone, I would go to a little chapel with Sister Catherine and say prayers. As silly as it sounds, I never forgot about God, and would also pray at night while I was falling asleep. It was a ritual. At that point I didn't have a keen awareness of God being in my life, but it seemed that it was what I was supposed to do.

The girl who had a room across from me was Hannah. We seemed to have a lot in common and laughed a lot together. We liked the same kind of music and we were both on a good course for a while. Hannah had been there for a few months already and was already going home on passes. I was on good behavior and doing everything I needed to do to get a weekend pass. Being there on the weekends was difficult.

My therapist was Ann Boyd. What a nerd. I would see her once a week either during or after school. She was a short woman with a blonde bob. You could tell that she probably had bad acne as a young person. Her eyes were tiny and dull blue. Ann hardly wore any make up; it probably would have helped if she had.

Ann didn't know much about drug addiction or alcoholism and was clueless about the streets. Nor did she seem to know about the difficulties that I faced when I was transplanted from Greece. So when I would go in for my therapy sessions she would want me to explain to her why I had been acting the way I had been. Well … I was just as stumped as she was at that point.

The hardest thing about that year or two were all the people who really didn't understand the agony I was feeling, which eventually led to my demise—addiction and rebelliousness. They hadn't experienced what I had. These were people who were trying to "help" me! Granted, they had probably read about certain behaviors in books. But if someone had come to me with some street smarts, or had a personal clue about what I was going through, it might have helped.

No one could relate to what I was feeling, which may be why I sought drugs and booze to derail me from my reality. When I wouldn't come home and I started running away, it was as if I had to; I needed to get high and drink. There became a point where it was not an option. I was disconnected from any choice; it was a thirst and hunger that consumed me. I had entered a whirlwind and became sucked down a toilet bowl. Initially, I was first delighting in a delectable feast, and then it all turned to shit.

I didn't like Ann Boyd. She was just like all the others.

FIFTEEN

Hannah and I were restless. Though she had weekend passes, she was restricted to her house and was having a rough time. More than anything, we wanted to get high. But I didn't have weekend passes, so we were contemplating going AWOL.

We talked about if for a while, and once the seed had been planted, there was no getting it out of our heads. What could I lose? I just wouldn't get my weekend passes for a while. Big deal! I wasn't going anywhere anyway! I was pretty sure I would be coming back to Shepherd Place. I could handle whatever happened.

We would go during the day when the unit wasn't locked, after school, or maybe when the unit meeting ended. We could slip out our door and down past the admissions desk. We wouldn't have much time before the police were called.

Hannah and I ran and went into Catonsville. Where in the hell were we? I had no idea. But she knew the area. We hitched a ride towards Baltimore. We went to her turf. I didn't want to go to mine after what had happened before. Besides, I knew we were far from Potomac.

I can remember being on Interstate 695 (the Baltimore Beltway), truck drivers, and being dropped off and picked up on ramps. It took us about three rides to get over to her area. I didn't know where I was. It's all hazy in my head.

We went to a house where Hannah knew someone and got high. It felt so good to get catch a buzz, to forget for a little while. I hadn't gotten high in a long time. It didn't matter where I was or who I was with. I wanted to block the world out.

Hannah and I stayed somewhere near Baltimore that night. We got obliterated on drugs and booze until morning. For a small space in time, I was in my mental paradise. But something came over me. I needed to go back. I couldn't keep running. It would have been only a matter of time before the cops would pick us up. I had been running for so long; it was time to just stop, at least physically.

We had someone drive us back to Shepherd Place. We were still buzzing when we got there. It's a horrible feeling to be high, searched, questioned, read the riot act, given "consequences," and then sent into the dorky therapist's office for an hour. Now that was torture!

Sister Catherine was not happy with us. I felt bad about letting her down and breaking her trust. It also tugged at me that I prolonged my "pass" privileges. Hannah lost her passes too.

Hannah ended up going AWOL again. She was gone for almost a week and we were all worried. I remember seeing her on return, as she was waiting to go and meet with the therapist. Hannah had that high and withdrawn look in her eyes, with dark circles underneath. I was so glad to see her but she was distant, and her stare went right through me. It was the last time I would see her for many years.

It was another thirty days before I was able to go home for a weekend. I could handle it. Shepherd Place was not that bad. The staff seemed fair and it actually seemed "humane." There was nobody trying to commit suicide or boys trying to rape you. There were some fights, but they actually broke up the boredom.

When my first weekend pass finally came, Mom and Dad picked me up. They were thrilled but nervous. I was so excited just to be in my own room and out of a "center." I would be good. And I was.

My weekend passes would go well for the most part; I was squeaky clean at the beginning. I really didn't want to blow it with the courts or my family. Still, my sisters were awkward around me, not that I blamed them, and it would be a long time before there was any healing between us all.

My sister Sheila came to pick me up from Shepherd Place one Friday. She had an old Dodge. We stopped at Arby's and got roast beef sandwiches. Sheila was reaching out. She didn't know any other way to do it but to come and get me and take me out for a sandwich. It meant a lot to my crippled spirit. We didn't say much. But I knew that she cared and that she probably knew it had been rough going for me. It had been tough for Sheila, too. It had been so hard for all of us, only in dissimilar ways. I'll never forget that day. Every time I see an Arby's, I think about Sheila and her meaningful gesture.

After a while, I would see old friends on my "weekends." Not a good idea. Before long I was getting high and drinking again. It seemed inevitable. I was an addict, and an alcoholic. It always felt so good to get rid of the pain, and now the guilt that was building.

I saw Tom. Sometimes he would drive me back to Shepherd Place and I would be high when I got there. Or I would have other friends drive me back. I had dated Pierre for a while. He was the cousin of Kerry, whose house had been broken into by Billy. His family owned a French Market in Georgetown. He was a gentleman, and that was foreign to me.

He and I would do other things besides get high or drink. We would go out to his father's country house and bring a picnic. Or we would go to the 75/80 race track in Urbana where he would race his Chevelle. It was the type of fun I hadn't experienced before. We actually did things besides just drink and drug.

Pierre's mother had died of cancer. His father had a mistress that lived with them. I don't think Pierre cared for her. This was a type of pain that I couldn't identify with. He felt for me and the predicament I was in. He seemed stumped, as so many people did. But he was sweet to me. I'll never forget that. We didn't last long.

My family was down at the beach for a week or two during the summer while I was at Shepherd Place, and I was able to go for a weekend. Sister Catherine drove me to the bus depot in Baltimore City and I took the Greyhound bus down to Ocean City where my parents and sisters picked me up. It was a long drive on the bus, and the weekend flew by quickly. I didn't want to leave the beach or my family.

Sister Catherine came to rely on me to help her with other girls. She called me a "trustee." I even went with her to retrieve a girl at her home who was refusing to come back. It was near the end of my stay and I think Sister felt like I could convince this girl that it wasn't worth screwing up. We did have luck getting the girl to come back. I guess if felt pretty good to help someone out in a positive way.

I actually did well at Shepherd Place. My stay lasted nine months, plus a few days. Before I got out, I had to go in front of Judge Tracy one final time. I think it was the fifth time I was dragged before him. He could see that I had improved my attitude and behavior dramatically. I had changed in many ways. He considered me a "success story," one of the few he had seen. He told me, "Patricia, I don't see many like you. You should be proud of yourself. I didn't have high hopes for you when you first came into my courtroom. I'm impressed. I hope the future is bright for you."

Those words meant a lot to me coming from Judge Tracy. I know he struggled with the decisions he had to make with regard to me. I did not envy his job and the power he held in his hands.

I got out of Shepherd Place and went home to a family that was hesitant to take me. My mom and dad wanted me to be "cured" and I wanted to be a "good" daughter. There were still weighty emotions that had not been mended. And the incarceration that I had just gone through had only added to the anguish I had initially suffered. The pain that I put my family through was not intentional. I truly loved my family; it was the fact that I loathed myself. I didn't blame them for being wary. My parents and sisters truly could not grasp what I had just gone through and how deeply addicted I had become to substances.

Still, I received no treatment.

SIXTEEN

was in contact with some of my old friends and went back to see some of my teachers at Cabin John Junior High. I even went to see a janitor whom I would drink with, Mr. Luther. He was the person who would console me sometimes in those days.

A lot of different things had been said about where I had been over the last year. I suppose in a way that wasn't surprising, but it took me a while to really absorb how such things had been said and who would have said them. Mr. Luther told me he had heard that I was prostituting down in Washington on Fourteenth Street. He had also heard I was dead. All of these rumors had weighed on him, for he cared about me and worried. He was one of the few people I could talk with, and he had always been there for me, reaching out when I needed help. He had never tried to hurt me or treat me in an inappropriate way. Still, if anyone had known about our relationship, Mr. Luther probably would have been fired.

It was decided that I would not go back to Churchill High School. I don't think I had a choice anyway. To return to my old stomping grounds and the same people just didn't seem wise. Despite the fact that I was hanging out with some of my old friends and easily lured back to drugs and alcohol, a new start seemed in order.

So I went to Charles W. Woodward High School. I knew one person, there, Eve. She was the daughter of one of my father's colleagues from the CIA. Eve was warm and welcoming. She introduced me to a lot of people and it helped. It was such a different experience than the one I had when we got to Potomac. But a lot of people got high and drank at Woodward.

Tom and I were still on and off. I think because we had a history together and my self-esteem was still so low, it was hard to get him out of my life. We continued to get into horrendous fights. One Christmas, he came to spend the holiday with my extended family and me. My parents were not thrilled with him, but I think they tried hard to accept, or tolerate, the people in my life.

Tom came into my grandparents' house to celebrate for a short while. He then asked me to come out to his truck with him before he drove up to West Virginia to his grandmother's house. We went out to his truck where he proposed marriage and gave me an engagement ring. I was not yet seventeen at the time. Wow, what a surprise that was! It made me happy that he was making this gesture. Maybe he really did want to spend the rest of his life with me and was going to treat me well.

I went back into the house and was ecstatic. I'll never forget the look on my parents' faces; I thought they were going to faint. I was so young. And Tom had treated me so repulsively. They were aghast. And why would he give me a ring and then just take off.

I made a lot of friends at Woodward. People accepted me easily. Again, it was not the best crowd, but I was able to stay out of any major trouble. I wasn't running away or stealing. I suppose to some degree that was a bit of an improvement.

Right before I turned seventeen, I got my driver's license. My instructor said I had a "lead foot." Mom and I would go out when I had my permit and we would get into terrible fights while she taught me to drive. Parallel parking with the big old station wagon was hardest. I was glad to be home and wanted to do well. But Mom and I were still struggling with each other. Obviously, I still had major issues to overcome. Mom just wanted me to be better. The truth of the matter was, I was "unwell."

My family tried to be there for me during my struggles. Of course I loved them and always will. But during those teenage years, I could not shake the edge that the drugs and booze had created. My attitude was wretched. I was smug. This made it near impossible for people around me.

I ended up buying a car with savings bonds that my Grandma Earnest had been giving me every year for my birthday. The bonds added up to five hundred dollars. I bought a 1972 Charger. It was green, and it went fast. Most of the kids in Potomac were driving brand new Camaros or BMWs that their parents would buy. If they wrecked them, their parents would buy them new ones.

The second car I bought was an Aspen R/T. It was black with red and orange racing stripes across the sides, and a spoiler. I thought it was so cool! When I bought it, I couldn't drive it off the lot because I didn't know how to drive a stick shift. Tom took me to a shopping center where he would put the car in "neutral" on a reclining hill until I could get it out of gear. I learned how to drive a manual vehicle in one night.

One of my good friends from Woodward, a girl named Tina, and I would get pretty drunk together. We would drink cheap wine, gallons of it. My tolerance for alcohol was so high; I needed to drink large amounts to get the buzz I wanted. Tina and I would get a little crazy together. We were out in Potomac one night and she wanted to ride on the roof of my car. Not a bright idea. I drove too fast and she fell off. She split her head open and was bleeding profusely. There was a group of us and we were all frantic, and drunk. Tina needed to go to the hospital and get stitches; there was no doubt. She didn't want to go. She was chicken.

We finally convinced her to go. So we got her to Suburban Hospital and she ran out. We were all running through the neighborhood at around 2:00 a.m., calling out her name. We eventually got her to go and she got her stitches.

Tina would get upset about the way Tom treated me. Sometimes she was there when we would fight and she would get in the middle. He and I would get drunk and physical. It wasn't pretty if someone tried to interfere, even if it was a friend trying to help. I'm sure I lost a lot of friends because of that relationship.

Tina introduced me to one of her friends, Shane, when Tom and I went over to his house one night to get some cocaine. Shane seemed to have a machismo that I was drawn to. We both seemed a bit taken with each other and I didn't care that Tom was there. I was getting over Tom anyway. At the time, Shane seemed on top of the world, at least in my eyes. He had a job in an auto body shop, shared a house with some buddies, drove a neat car, and was dealing. He was good looking and his attitude was that he didn't care what people thought. My engagement with Tom was history, and Shane and I started going out. On our first date, I waited for him at his house while he was on his way back from a day in the mountains. He was late. And when he got there he was tripping on acid, so basically he was hysterically laughing for about two or three hours. It was humorous at the time.

One of Shane's friends worked as a manager at a bank in Bethesda. We would go and meet up with him when he would close up the bank. After he locked up the bank, we would get high inside. It somehow seemed thrilling.

Shane and I had a lot of fun during the short time that we were together. He was good to me, in my eyes. We drank, did a lot of drugs and there often were a lot of people at his house. He was a charmer, and my parents actually liked him.

On my seventeenth birthday, Shane and a friend of ours named Candy drove down to Ocean City. They were going to drive some BMWs back for her boyfriend who worked at the dealership. We drove one car down together and partied the whole way. We picked up the cars on schedule. Shane and Candy were both driving fast, at least 80-90 mph. As we passed Salisbury and were going through a stretch of clear highway on Route 50, the police lights came on. But the car went up towards Candy who was in front of us and so he was in between our car and hers. He pulled both of us over.

None of us liked cops. It was distressing to me to get pulled over. Shane and Candy were both nasty and uncooperative. I was just along for the ride. It was obvious they were under the influence. So they were arrested for speeding and DUI. I had to go to the jail with them because basically I was stuck down there. I waited the whole night until Candy's boyfriend came and they had sobered up. I slept on a bench in the waiting room at the police station.

When we all got back in the cars to come back to town, Candy went back up to 80 mph like a moron.

Shane would get possessive and he wasn't extremely attentive. I knew he cared deeply for me but, despite my having a big heart for him, there were some things that soured me on the relationship. When I did part ways with him, he did not take it well. We had been at a party and Shane ended up taking my car, saying he was going to get cigarettes. He parked my car somewhere mysteriously. He then went to his house and passed out. Some of Shane's roommates actually helped me look for him and my car. When we finally caught up to him all we got was stubborn laughter and he said I would have to wait until the next day to get my car. Then he rolled over and went back to sleep.

Within several weeks, Shane showed up at my place of work. He wanted to say goodbye, since he was joining the Marine Corps. We stayed in touch and tried dating again several times. There was just something about him. We have remained friends.

<hr>

I never thought about how my lifestyle would affect my job or get me in trouble with the law. Like an idiot, I still hung out with old friends from Potomac. Christine would come in and out of my life, even though she was an abrasive person. We always spurred each other on due to our common bond with booze and drugs.

One night we were hanging out in Potomac. I don't know what it was about Potomac that I felt lured by; it was as if I had a love/hate relationship with the town. And I did not consciously think about possible trouble with the law, even after everything I had been through. Some friends (or associates rather), that we knew from Cabin John were there too. Dan and Mike needed a ride somewhere.

We gave them a ride because they had joints we could smoke on the way. Little did we know that Dan was under surveillance by some undercover cops because he had gone onto his mother's property after she had a restraining order against him. There was a warrant out for his arrest for trespassing. We drove for awhile, unaware that we were being followed. As we were driving, we were speeding and smoking pot.

Before we crossed a one-lane bridge down on MacArthur Boulevard in Glen Echo, four or five cop cars surrounded us and their lights went on. A loud speaker went on with a voice saying, "Everyone out of the car with their hands up in the air!" The cops got out and pointed their guns at us. We were told to put our hands against the car. I kept asking what was going on, since I had no idea, and we were told to just do as we were told and then they'd let us know what the situation was. Then the cops asked if Dan Weaver was there. And I got pissed. I said, "Okay Dan, what did you do?" Dan played dumb well, or maybe he really WAS a dumbass. So he said, "I went to my old folks and I wasn't supposed to. Big shit, I needed to get some clothes."

Meanwhile, Mike's face was being pushed against the pavement of the road because he was having a fit and giving the cops a hard time. So I started getting mad because it was a perplexing situation, and the policemen started saying something about the drugs that they saw us smoking as they were following us. I was a bit worried. But I was high at the time and really pissed at these cops. I was really annoyed with Dan. I just didn't need this.

It was a total fiasco at the police station. I always got a bit scrappy once the cuffs went on. Plus, with Christine, Mike, and Dan there, we were all feeding off of each other. I think I had a bottle of perfume in my purse that I sprayed in the station, saying that it "really smelled." It did not help the situation.

I did have to go to court and Mr. Topping, my old lawyer, represented me. Mom and Dad were not happy, to say the least. By this time I was eighteen, so I was being charged as an adult. Because Dan was wanted by the police and he was in my car, I was "harboring" him. But then the drug use and possession charge was added into the whole mess.

The funny thing about it all is Dan showed up in court in torn jeans and a T-shirt, not caring at all about his predicament. Whereas I had been down such a bad road before with the courts, I was nervous. I felt lousy about disappointing my parents too. This was a rancid reminder of where I had been before. I didn't want to go back.

The charges got dropped, as long as I kept my nose clean for a certain length of time. Mom and Dad probably paid Mr. Topping a bit of money for representing me. I was unaware and unappreciative at the time.

To my amusement, Christine went off and joined the circus. Her home and Potomac were so unbearable for her that she tried to get as far away as possible. She was gone for almost a year and ended up living with a horse trainer. We didn't stay in touch much longer after her return.

I made it through high school by the skin of my teeth. I basically had missed my eighth, ninth, and part of tenth grade, due to all the drugs, drinking, running away, and eventual incarceration. I had no high GPA or huge accomplishments to brag about. I don't even think I took the SATs. But I graduated. It was a monumental event. Mom and Dad were proud. I don't think they ever thought the day would come. We celebrated with a party for me, and my ceremony was at Cole Field House on the University of Maryland campus. It was long and boring, but noteworthy.

Apart from that, there were no memorable days or nights to look back on during this dark period of my life. I never went to a homecoming dance or to the prom. And, years later, I never went to any of my high school reunions. Because my time at both Churchill and Woodward high schools were short lived, I made few long lasting connections with people that I really wanted to stay in touch with. Sadly, I was recreating the disjointed friendships that I experienced as a child from all the traveling and then substance abuse.

SEVENTEEN

Mom and Dad didn't talk much to my sisters and me about school, aspirations and going out into the great big world. Realistically, I didn't feel prepared for what was out there after graduation. I had been working part time in a medical consulting firm, running big jobs on the Xerox machine and making deliveries. I worked there for more than three years and made decent money, but I eventually got bored.

I went to Bartending School after I left that company. I had odd jobs as a waitress here and there, but I assumed that I could make more as a bartender. I also had jobs as a nanny and volunteered as a Big Sister to a teenage girl going through the court system.

This was about the time that my mother left my father, in 1980, one year after I had graduated from high school.

Mom sat us all down in the living room of the Potomac house. Nancy and Sheila were both dating young men at the time. Carol was the only one still living at home.

Mom said she wasn't happy and needed some "time to think." She was going to go away for a little while. It was confusing, but okay. She was gone for about a month. Mom came back and again, sat us all down in the living room. She said that she was in a relationship and leaving for good. Mom said that she loved this person, and then told us that this person just happened to be a woman. Whoa!

I think I laughed, and then I cried. How do you react to such news? Nobody could say the "L-word." Nobody could say anything for a long time. We were speechless. Dad was devastated.

It was just Dad and Carol at the house in Potomac. Carol was depressed. She was in her last year of high school and barely hanging in there. Together, she and Dad were like two lost pups.

I would go to the house and see Dad home from work with his martini. It was all he could do to keep it together. He adored Mom and I know he didn't see it coming. They had tried counseling.

It didn't seem like a lot of people divorced at that time. Maybe they did, but I felt like nobody else was going through what I was or could understand. It was perplexing. I thought Mom and Dad were happy.

I remembered the fight that I had overheard my parents having when we were living in Rockville. But that had been long ago and it had seemed like everything was fine between them now.

There are many theories about how children handle divorce. Some professionals believe that children may blame themselves. I never felt responsible for my parents' divorce. But I did question what was "real" or genuine about their marriage. How far back did the unhappiness go? It felt like more betrayal.

I started dating Ricardo, another loser. It seemed that when it came to men, I was always selling myself short. What he lacked in personality, he made up for in looks. He was quite beautiful, but he knew it. He had Italian and Colombian blood, which gave him an olive complexion. Often he had a five o'clock shadow that I thought was sexy as hell. His eyes were deep brown but tainted. You could see a scarred life the minute you looked into them. Of course, we fancied getting high and drinking together. He was an ex-junkie, but said that he had stopped shooting long ago when he moved away from Bogotá, Columbia, where his family had lived.

I knew Ricardo through a friend of Tom's. His name was Evan, and we had done cocaine together. "White" seduced me like no other drug. Evan had a cool Challenger and it was gorgeous. (I think it was 72.) He and Tom would race, and Evan could beat him sometimes. I liked that.

During this time, Ricardo and I were living together in an apartment in Rockville. I had only stayed at home for a year or two after graduating.

Ricardo and I indulged in a lot of drugs and booze together. Numbing out was always the status quo for me. I didn't see it as a problem, or want to figure it all out. Ricardo had a huge ego. At times he was a gym rat and his physique was something he was quite consumed with. I started working out and going to the gym as well. Oddly, on the one hand while we were taking such good care of our bodies; on the other hand we were destroying ourselves. I was jogging about three miles a day and working out in the gym. I was careful about what I ate. I got maniacal about food. I didn't like to eat meat at all because it gave me morose thoughts at the time. I decided I wanted to try and go vegetarian. Being thin was important, almost an obsession.

We loved going to the clubs dancing. I'll admit, Ricardo was quite a dancer, but he was a bit of a hotshot. He danced like Mick Jagger and was a wannabe. He came to my sister Sheila's wedding and my dad would comment about how great Ricardo was on his feet. The guy didn't need his head inflated any more than it already was.

One day, I got a call from Ricardo in Suburban Hospital. He had been hit by a car while standing at a bus stop on the side of the road near his parent's home in Potomac. Both of his legs had been broken.

I wasn't sure what to expect when I got to the hospital. He was lying on the gurney and seemed in okay spirits with his chiseled chest exposed but legs covered. There was fear and despair in his eyes. Sadly, despite how lucky he was, he knew that physically he would never be the same, even at that moment. How quickly our lives can change, in the flash of one moment. It really is true.

The man who hit Ricardo claimed that he was a diabetic and that he had gone into insulin shock. That may have been true, but it was his third accident and he left the scene. Ricardo was able to get a settlement. It was done rather quickly. I think he got approximately $60,000. Ricardo started dealing coke with the money. He would buy large quantities of the drug, then cut it with a powdered laxative or vitamin that weakened its potency. This allowed Ricardo to make a profit and for us to use more cocaine. Our habits became monstrous. We would stay up for days snorting coke and not eating, bathing or sleeping. The insanity that came over our mind was indescribable. Ricardo would shoot up sometimes and he wanted me to do so as well. I didn't want to put a needle in my arm, and never did.

At the time, I had a job as a waitress downtown. One of my good friends, Bill, would come over to get coke and party with us. He was gay, and his lover took issue with me. The fact that Bill and I hung out so much together seemed to make his partner quite insecure.

Bill and I would serve champagne brunch at the restaurant, and of course we always had a bottle hidden for ourselves somewhere. We would get half drunk during the shift and it was our secret, our demented fun. Sometimes we would even do white at the restaurant; I would bring a "bullet" of coke with me for easy access. It helped get us get through the shift. Eventually, we would venture to my house and do cocaine. Bill liked to shoot up and didn't want to make me uncomfortable. So he would go into another room, do his thing and then we would all enjoy our high together.

Several years later I saw Bill's name on a list of people who had succumbed to AIDS. At that time, the disease was prevalent in the gay community. I loved Bill dearly and missed him terribly.

Ricardo started getting bizarre sexually. We had friends that we partied with regularly, Beth and Mark. Beth was cute with short brown hair and big, brownish, puppy-like eyes. She was tall and worked as a waitress. She had a sweet figure. Mark was handsome with blonde hair and blue eyes. He was not extremely masculine in my opinion. Apparently Ricardo, Mark and Beth had all talked about "switching" partners and how erotic this would be. I had no interest in partaking; it was too extreme and kinky. But one night we were all extremely high and they persuaded me into fulfilling their fantasy.

It started out rather innocently with us playing strip poker. Slowly, our clothes started coming off. This became spicy as cocaine often made us aroused. I know the guys wanted to see the two of us girls get together but it just didn't go that way. Mark approached me and started fondling me; it was exciting and mysterious. He picked me up and took me to another room. I would be with Mark and Beth would have sex with Ricardo. It felt foreign and strange. We were all in the same vicinity of each other. This made it more awkward. Hearing every noise and sound was one thing. But then Ricardo proceeded to make comments across the room to Mark. Ricardo would say to Mark, "She's good isn't she?"

Mark would reply, "Oh yeah!"

Beth quietly let Ricardo screw her. I could hear him going in and out of her. He told her how soft her skin was.

Mark was all atwitter and shaking. I couldn't tell if it was because Beth and Ricardo were in the room next to us or because this was such a sensual experience for him. He told me how beautiful I was. His touch was delicate and he moved slowly into me. In that moment, I yearned for love, a sweet caress. My thoughts were so contorted and twisted from the drugs. Mark's eyes seemed to search for something far inside mine. I knew there was only emptiness.

After that night, things were never the same between the four of us, as might be predicted. But Mark now wanted to meet with me secretly. He seemed to have a hard time accepting the word no. And Beth became insecure about their relationship. Nothing good came out of it.

Abstractly, I felt as though Black Cupid had pierced me. There was a deep, tar filled hole inside me that was impossible to fill. As much as I tried to stimulate my mind with drugs, booze and now dark sex, I couldn't. I felt an immense, ominous fog descend over my world and I couldn't escape.

The night with Beth and Mark seemed to be a segue for Ricardo and his ferocious sexual appetite. We would get extremely high and he would want to bring other men home from bars and watch them with me. Ricardo needed more intimate stimulation as we were doing larger amounts of drugs. We would get so coked that it didn't matter to me at that point what we did. Sex was always a part of us using "white."

He would go out to a bar and select someone. It seemed so easy for Ricardo to entice someone back to our apartment. I'm not sure what exactly he told them would happen. These men would follow Ricardo in his car and he would drive indirectly to our abode so they didn't know exactly how they had gotten there. Obviously, they would have figured it out somehow if they wanted to. They were allowed to consume some of our drugs, which I'm sure was part of the appeal. I was not allowed to see them. I assumed and hoped in my mind that they had an acceptable appearance. Always, I would conjure up a picture in my mind of what these men looked like. Before these strangers entered the room, Ricardo would blindfold me with a bandana. He allowed them to undress me if they desired to do so; usually I would have lingerie on, which made it seductive. Ricardo (and I) allowed them to touch me anywhere. They could not kiss my lips. I would get extremely aroused. Ricardo would let these unfamiliar men unclothe themselves and rub against me. They could not penetrate me. I remember hearing one of them say he wanted Ricardo to join along, so possibly this person was bi-sexual. Eventually, Ricardo would tell them when it was time for them to leave. They would then follow him out the same way they came in. I realized later, how warped (and risky) these encounters were. There were not many; it didn't matter.

I had betrayed my physical spirit. In spite of these wretched exploits and all the drugs, I was able to disconnect from my body and what I had allowed myself to do. I had plummeted to a new, degrading low for myself. But later in time these trysts seemed to evoke emotions that were difficult to put behind me for years. The shame continued to poison my being. Even after Ricardo and I parted ways, it took many years to have normal sexual relations with anyone. For a long time, I would wonder if someone was creeping into my bedroom. There had been a distorted view of sex created by the drugs and booze. I felt like scum.

Ricardo and I reached a point where reality was almost completely lost to us. A lot of paranoia came with using cocaine. We would binge every day and night. Ricardo was sure that the police were watching the house or coming to get us. Or, he was worried that someone would break in to get the drugs when there were large quantities. At times, there would be several ounces of cocaine where we lived. He would constantly pace and look out the windows, which were always covered. When we would try and get to sleep, it would take hours even after coming down from the coke. We would smoke a lot of pot and drink to help our buzz wear off. Coming off the buzz from coke was agonizing; we just wanted to do more. We felt like vampires that lived for the drug. We hated when daylight came and the sounds of the world rising would remind us that we were still high on coke.

We didn't want to think about "normal" people getting on with their lives. All we thought about was scoring more drugs. It was a dreaded feeling, pure drudgery. I would long for the darkness to return and basically that's how our abode was—blackness. There were times when I could not discern between dawn and dusk. Sometimes our stomachs would be so sick from the drugs and not eating for days that we couldn't keep anything down. We were becoming skin and bones. Our complexions looked haunted from not going out in the sunshine.

According to lab experiments, rats will choose cocaine over food, drink, or sleep until they die. At that point, my using was so bad that I may as well have thrown myself in front of a speeding train.

There were nights when Ricardo and I would drive his friend Fabio downtown, to Southeast DC, to get high. Fabio would want to get Dilaudid; he liked heroin but was also using this very powerful and expensive narcotic. It was always easy to find a corner where we could score; how safe it was is another story. Fabio scored a few pills that looked like Dilaudids. Guys would come up to the car window, show you a glimpse of the goods, grab your cash and run. After this young black guy was long out of sight, Fabio pulled out his works to shoot up. He took a good look at what he had gotten. He knew it wasn't the real thing, but he so desperately wanted to get high that he shot it up anyway. Ricardo and I just puffed on a joint as we listened to Fabio in agony, waiting to fall into a euphoric high that never came.

We were renting a basement apartment from my mother's companion, Miranda, above Georgetown, so my mom and Miranda could hear us sometimes. Apparently, there was one night that there was a lot of screaming going on. I don't remember that night at all; my mother told me about it later. It was late. My mom and Miranda came down and burst through the door to see what all the chaos and noise was about. What they saw was Ricardo trying to shoot me up with a syringe. We were both out of our minds on drugs. Mom and Miranda told Ricardo to "get the hell out!" He seemed to know that his life was probably in jeopardy if he didn't.

I do recall fighting with Ricardo about the drugs and not having enough money for us to keep up with our binges. He had already been "cutting" the coke more and more so it decreased the purity of what was being sold to customers. That left more for us, but even then we were frantic about how we would get coke when the money had run out. Ricardo had spent his whole settlement by then, as well as the money from the dealing he was doing. All the money had gone to cocaine and pot within months –- more than $50,000.00 plus cash that he had made dealing! We were doing over a quarter ounce on some days, at least.

The only thing I remember beyond the night that Ricardo left was sleeping in the attic for days. I slept but didn't eat. My mother would check on me. It was all a big, cloudy haze.

Years later I heard that Sheila, my beloved, unselfish sister, had gone in and cleaned my apartment. It's hard to tell what it looked like or what she found. Who knows what she was thinking as she was going through the remains of two insane drug addicts. I love her for her kindness.

Basically, at that point my family knew I had a substance abuse problem. My family all met in Miranda and Mom's living room to have an "intervention." That's what it might be called now, although from what I've read and been told about a typical intervention, this was not a formal type. There was no specialist. When each person would speak to me or address me, they would say how much damage I had caused to them in the past and that they weren't willing to go through that again.

⸎

In retrospect, there was no question I had caused a lot of pain and damage to my family. But there was obviously a tremendous amount of turmoil going on inside of me that needed to be addressed. I just didn't know who to get help from or how to go about doing so. I was like a lost puppy crying out in so many ways, but my addiction was being deflected and destroying my life.

I do remember one thing that I said to my father during that meeting. I asked him if he could please tell me that he loved me every now and then. He agreed.

There was no plan agreed on per se, but it was made clear that I needed to get help and I agreed. I wasn't sure how I was going to go about doing it, but Mom was going to help. I didn't see booze as a problem. Cocaine was my problem. In my mind, I could control my drinking.

I knew that there was no way I was going into a hospital or rehab. I refused to check myself into any sort of place after all the time that I had spent in institutions and detention centers. I would create my own program instead. So, Mom made appointments for me with different psychiatrists. I hated going and talking. One of them, after listening for a while, proceeded to tell me about his coke problem. Great, maybe he should have been lying on the couch and I could have sat on the chair and taken notes.

Along with seeking help, I also decided to quit my job as a waitress and get a new one. I worked in Johnson's Flower Shop on Wisconsin Avenue in Chevy Chase. It was a pleasant change of pace. I loved being around all the plants and flowers. It smelled like a spring morning every day and people were happy to be there; it was a cheery environment. The pay stunk, but that wasn't my main motivation.

I also decided to volunteer in a Montessori school. This was a school where there were children with special needs and horseback riding was used as a therapeutic method for reaching them. It was exhilarating to work there and to help others.

There was a wonderful woman that we came across named Jackie Fey. She was a hypnotherapist. I liked her. She was a black woman who seemed genuine, perceptive and "with it." I liked that.

It was a pleasure to work with Jackie. I felt like I could talk to her about things that had torn at my heart for a long time, things that I had been running from in one way or another. It was clear that my self-esteem had become an issue through the years. I had gotten into relationships with abusive men. I had destroyed my future in many ways by doing so poorly in school.

Jackie was the first person that I ever worked with who helped me identify some of my core issues. It never consciously occurred to me that I might be upset over my parents' divorce. Or, that I may have had some pent up feelings over the fact that my mom was gay and never voiced because I was too busy getting high and drunk. It seemed there was a lot of grief over the fact that Greece had been my home for so long and then I had to adjust to life in the United States. That had been extremely difficult for me, and it just hadn't felt at all welcoming when I came here. I wanted to go back in time. My wish was to go in reverse and fly back to where I came from. If only I could have started all over. But there was no going back.

In hypnotherapy I was dealing with painful topics in my subconscious mind. I wasn't aware of this torment on the surface. If I were cognizant, surely I wouldn't have told anyone. I was quite busy building a tough wall to mask it. I had little recollection of what came up in therapy with Jackie. I didn't know how to put an end to the abusive relationships with men. And I felt hindered with shame and guilt.

When a person begins doing drugs and drinking heavily, their age is stunted at that time. So basically, since I had started indulging in drugs and booze at around 14 or 15, I remained that age mentally and emotionally until I could stop abusing those substances. At the time I was seeing Jackie, I was in my twenties.

Eventually, I came up with some goals for myself. I had never had any ambitions. We talked about my going to college, which at first seemed so inconceivable. But the more I thought about it, why not?

First, I had to decide what I wanted to do with my life. This was not easy. I had never thought in these terms. I had never looked to the future. In my eyes, I wasn't going to live that long because I was living such a subversive life. Possibly, there was a corner in my heart and mind that didn't want to live long as it was anyway.

I wanted to work with people. We talked about nursing school, social work, teaching, and other possible career paths At that point, I came up with physical therapy as a major to take in school. I could go to a community college, work hard, bring up my GPA, and then transfer to a university that offered my major.

I was ecstatic! I was going to go to college! I was going to make a real life for myself. I was almost becoming normal.

EIGHTEEN

My father always promised to pay for half our college and that offer still stood. But I had to come up with other money, which was not going to be easy. I would waitress that summer and save. I got a job at Gusti's downtown on Nineteenth and M streets in D.C. I worked the lunch and dinner shifts six or seven days a week. I saved five thousand dollars that summer.

But I was still drinking. And I drank a lot that summer because all I did was work. I was so tired that by the time I was off, there seemed to be no time for anything else. So I would go out with everyone from work and drink. Or I would do shots at the bar in between my shifts. This started to become a dire habit.

One weekend, I had an actual day off and my sister Nancy and I decided to drive to Chesapeake Bay. We liked to go down there, be near the water and scout for sharks' teeth. As we were driving down, my stomach started hurting terribly. It worsened progressively. Nancy suggested we pull over to a 7-11 and maybe get some Rolaids or a soda.

I could barely walk into the store, the pain was so unbearable. People actually thought I was drunk, and this was one of the rare occasions that I wasn't. The pain was so bad that Nancy decided to take me to the hospital near where we were. I dragged myself into the emergency room and plopped myself on a chair, moaning. Nancy checked me in.

My mom was near the bay too, so Nancy called and she showed up at the hospital.

I was put on a gurney in a little room surrounded by curtains. The doctor came in and asked me a bunch of questions. They decided to give me an abdominal x-ray and inject fluids through an IV. They poked me repeatedly to get the IV in and it hurt. It was the first time I had ever had an IV and the needles were thick.

The X-ray showed that I had kidney stones. The doctor said I would probably "pass" them on my own when I urinated and gave me a screen to pee through every time I went to the bathroom. He said if I could catch it to bring it into an urologist for an analysis. It might indicate why I had the kidney stones.

I tried to "catch" the stones for about a week to no avail. I can assure anyone who has not had them that kidney stones are extremely painful.

So that was how I spent one of the few days off that I had that summer.

At Gusti's we would balance trays on our shoulders as we went up and down stairs. Sometimes, we would have as many as six to eight plates on the trays. And there was an outside cafe at the restaurant, so during the summer months, it was hot. The temperature sometimes topped 100 degrees. Then there was the humidity! Many "swampy" areas surrounding DC make the air thick.

It was difficult watching all the diners having fun and being merry while I was busting my butt, especially on holidays like the Fourth of July when we would get packed. Most evenings, I wouldn't get out of there until around 2:00 or 3:00 in the morning.

There was also a little bit of dealing with the homeless population in the sense that they would harass our customers who were sitting in the outdoor café. They would ask them for money. Or, every now and then we would get one that would come in, eat, and then run out on the check. Honestly, there were some who looked like "normal" people; you couldn't always tell. But when they ran out on the check, the manager would want us as employees to pay for it, so it was deducted from our tips. This seemed unfair.

One crazy woman ran in and out of the traffic, trying to get hit by the cars. Rumor had it that she had been hit twice already. She would go to the psychiatric hospital, but only stay there for three days. Apparently she had kids, but had lost custody of them because she was so mentally unstable. Obviously, she needed to be on medication. Maybe she could have been somewhat stable if she took meds regularly. There were a lot of people like that in the city.

One day, I finished my lunch shift and went to the bar where the bartender was a friend. I started drinking and then doing tequila shots—not a wise decision. I got extremely smashed before it was time for me to return to work. I was supposed to work the dinner shift. I tried waiting on tables and I was practically falling over the customers. I was slurring my speech. The manager pulled me aside. He told me that I needed to leave for the evening. I was devastated. Was he firing me? I had been such a good employee. How could he do this to me!

All I remember was wandering out into the streets of DC in turmoil. I was drunk, exhausted, and confused. I'm sure people were avoiding me as I stumbled past, but I don't remember. The only thing I recall was waking up on the pavement face up. What I saw was a crowd gathered around me and several paramedics checking me. I had cuts on me that were bleeding and my clothes were a bit torn in places. My clothes were still on, thank God!

I seemed to be okay, other than dazed and shaken up. A cab was called for me because I had no idea where my car was and I was in no condition to drive. It was the day of my worst blackout. But it was not the first or last. I did not find my car for days.

Fortunately, I did still have my job. I decided not to do shots in between shifts at work, although it was tempting. Despite that episode, I still didn't see the drinking as a problem.

It was also at that time that my father started dating Sharon. She was a bit younger than he, but they seemed compatible. I think it was difficult for dad to be alone, but he did not rush into a relationship immediately.

I wasn't sure what to think of Sharon at first. Certainly, I was consumed with other things in my life. She was not overbearing in any way, and allowed me to accept her in my own time. She was respectful and eventually became a wonderful part of the family.

I signed up for classes at Northern Virginia Community College. It was a good school for me to raise my grades, get a high GPA, and transfer to a university. I took basic classes, plus I was working and paying for the apartment in Georgetown.

My motivation to do well was high. I loved school. Before I got there, I had filled out massive amounts of paperwork to get student loans and grants. I was given a grant almost every semester I attended.

Unfortunately, my math skills were so poor that I had to take prep courses before I could take the actual college credit classes. So I was taking math classes that I was paying for and working hard at, but they were high school math courses. Even so, I found them difficult.

I made wonderful friends at NVCC. They were straight, academic people. It was quite a change, but refreshing. One of my good friends was Jay, a young Korean man who helped me with my math. He was studying to be a med student. He was impressively intelligent and willing to help, which I appreciated. Jay literally tutored me for hours. When I would have an exam come up, I think he would get more nervous than I. He would come and wait outside my class anxiously wondering how I did. His help during that time was priceless.

I got almost straight A's in all my classes. I took school seriously. I joined the Student Government Association and actually got a Merit Award for my grades and community service. I even entered one of my poems in a poetry contest and won second prize. I was also awarded one of America's Most Outstanding Women in Junior Colleges. It was all too surreal to get such recognition and positive feedback; it was foreign to me. My parents were proud.

But math remained a difficult subject for me. I think that missing such a huge foundation of math with all the moving around when I was younger hindered my ability to understand the concepts. Then I really blew it by skipping school and dropping out. I could make up for all the other subjects, except for math.

Jay and I would go to the library for hours and hours. Sometimes, we would go to George Mason or George Washington Universities, because they had better material for us to look up or with which to do research projects. They had better study rooms at their libraries too. I did whatever I needed to in order to excel.

For a while, I was only going to school, studying, and working a job at a restaurant called Summer's. I would change jobs frequently. I was experiencing success for the first time in many years. It was actually the first time I had achieved any goals as an adult. My classes were going extremely well except, of course, math. I made it through college math and to pre-calculus. By the time I got to physics, I was really struggling. Jay was trying to help me, but to no avail. My obsession with getting at least a B in that class was getting the best of me; nothing else was acceptable. I had put a lot of pressure on myself.

But there was other pressure as well. The major I had chosen was competitive at the time. If I wanted to get into a good university and my major was Physical Therapy, my grades had to be up to par. I had a decision to make. It would probably be necessary to drop out of Physics and change my major. I was devastated. I actually became suicidal.

This was the first time I had a goal for myself and had experienced some positive success in my life! And now I felt like I had to let it go. Even though it wasn't over and I could reinvent everything, I felt like a part of me had failed. In my mind, I couldn't be successful, and I would never accomplish anything.

For the time being, I made my major English Literature until I decided what I definitely wanted to do. But during that time I was emotionally vulnerable and did a bit of drinking. School was important, but I started hanging with people that were a little different than the academic people that had been my companions while academically focused.

⌗

There was a place in Great Falls, Virginia, that I liked going to because the police couldn't get to it easily and I could be out in nature. A lot of people would gather there and party. I gravitated toward a group of people that introduced me to the place and I became a regular.

We would jump off the high cliffs into the river or dive under the big boulders in the middle of the water and end up in an underwater cave. There was a rock formation in the center of the water that created a tunnel. You could "ride" the water through as the strong current carried you. The danger was seductive.

I would bring beer or liquor to drink, and soon the drugs began to call to me again as well. There was a guy I could buy pot from who was always around. He was kind of creepy, but he would always have something to get buzzed on, even acid sometimes. It was there that I met Ben, a handsome, cocky, law student from Pennsylvania who drank like a fish and liked to get high too.

Ben came on to me pretty instantly. But I actually was not interested in his company from the get-go. I think at that point I was enjoying my independence and had an unconscious awareness that men had been toxic to my well being. But I did give him my phone number. I thought maybe he would be different since he was in school—law school, no less!

He called. I think I avoided him for a day or two. But I ended up going to his house where I met his three roommates. A nice first date! We hung out and partied and then went downtown to hit the bars. The bar scene in DC in the 80's was stimulating. There were always lines to get into the popular places. You could get any drug, meet a lot of people, and dance the night away.

Ben and I started seeing each other regularly. He was tall and muscular. Ben had dirty blonde hair, high cheekbones and intense, penetrating hazel eyes. He had gorgeous lips and was a killer kisser. Yes, we liked to party together. One night he was in my apartment in Georgetown and mentioned cocaine. I told him I used to do it but gave it up. He wanted to know if I knew where we could score some. Of course I did. I was trying to be good, but weakening quickly.

Once the word had been mentioned it was hard to get the idea out of my head. The trigger was in motion. I was craving coke badly now. We were pretty tipsy as it was. I thought Ben would be amusing to snort coke with. Surprisingly, I was good that night and we abstained. But I obsessed over it and the next time we got together we decided to get some.

So I was back to doing cocaine in addition to the drinking and pot smoking. Ben was not a real prince; he was like all the others. He didn't like to pay when we went out and he would put me down a lot, saying that he was joking. Sometimes, I would just not take his calls or plan something with a friend rather than see him. My soul felt battered and he only hammered away at it more.

Ben had a friend named Scott who was a real sweetheart. He and I had great conversations and liked to party too. I think he had a huge crush on me, but I wasn't attracted to him and I was dating Ben. But sometimes when I would tire of Ben, Scott and I would get a hotel room in town and just party. We were not intimate in anyway. We just liked to party and talk. We liked writing poetry together and going for walks. It was an elegant respite from someone that I had become attached to that wasn't treating me respectfully. Ben thought Scott and I were having intimate relations.

I was not born with half a brain. I had just never gained much confidence in myself. All my pride had been slowly chipped away beginning with all the different schools from the traveling back and forth, the eventual move to Potomac, the drugs, booze, my parents' divorce, my want for more from my father emotionally, my mothers' lifestyle, and all the hardhearted men that I dated. It's like a sculptor with his creation. Only I started as this golden haired, innocent girl and was transformed into something ugly. I felt so flawed in numerous ways.

NINETEEN

I was so attracted by Ben's looks that it took me a little while to figure out that he was a jerk. I also discovered that he liked to wear my lingerie. He felt sexy in my panties. As I inquired into this kinky behavior of his, he divulged that he wasn't sure if he was bi-sexual and that he had an older man in Ohio who helped pay for his education. He was never completely honest with me about whether he had sexual relations with this man. Ben seemed ashamed, but I was blown away. It really wasn't what I signed on for, especially after the whole Ricky situation.

When I broke up with him, he didn't take it well. He called a lot. He also just showed up at my house uninvited. On one occasion, my old flame Shane and I were going out on his Harley and Ben followed us for awhile. Sometimes I would allow him to stay at my place when he came over and other times I would have plans and turn him away. One night, he stayed when he was drunk (which was usually the case). He actually passed out in my bed. I had to work the next day and I left him there. When I got home he was gone, but he had left me a nice little surprise. He had urinated all over my bed and just turned the mattress over.

The only way I knew this was because when I left that morning, I knew he had pissed all over himself through the night from being so drunk and out of it. When I left he was semi-conscious and had a Cheshire cat like look on his face as I was leaving. It was a look that said, "yeah, I'm lying in pee right now, and there's not really much I can do about it, but hopefully you don't know."

That was pretty much the last straw with Ben. But he wouldn't stop calling or coming over. He was harassing me.

At that point, I had transferred to the University of Maryland, or was in the midst of doing so. Getting accepted was a huge deal to me. Ben was becoming a distraction I could not avoid or afford.

One night, we argued so loudly that Mom heard us from upstairs. She came down in tears. She didn't know if I was high or being hurt. It was like déjà vu for her. I assured her that I was fine; it was simply an argument and that I had everything under control. I felt like I did, and that I could handle the situation. But Ben was persistent.

So, I moved. I went to Greenbelt, into a townhouse near College Park, Maryland, where my university was, so I could get to school easily. My phone number and address would be different. I rented from a man named John, who was partially paralyzed from a disease he was born with. There was another girl who lived there. She liked to party too and she had a boyfriend.

Though I didn't think Ben had my number or knew where I lived, somehow he found out where I lived and drove there one night. He just showed up in his usual manner. I was shocked, But I suppose there was a part of me that wasn't surprised. I felt harassed and invaded.

Basically, I drowned myself in schoolwork. I did well. There was a part of me that became frustrated with "the system." When I got to Maryland, they wouldn't accept all my credits from NVCC and so I had to take some basic classes over. Not only was this costly in terms of tuition, but it consumed my time too.

I liked Maryland. It was a beautiful campus and felt extremely academic. For the first time, I was exposed to fraternity houses and sororities. But I was older and the other students seemed young. They seemed a bit immature to me. But they were quite serious about their groups, what they stood for, and the whole system.

Despite my being studious, I was fighting the impulse to party.

I got a job at a deli in Hyattsville, Maryland. It was not the best part of town, but the owner was willing to let me work around my class schedule. The job was close to the campus and my townhouse. My job was to run the lottery machine and he said I would be busy. I was.

It was interesting working at the deli. Everybody that worked there was laid back, which I liked. There was always a line out the door for people to come in and run their numbers hoping to win the lotto. The regulars gambled a lot, and it was obvious they didn't have extra money to spend. My boss, Tad, told me that some of them were spending their social security checks on the lottery. It made me sad.

There were only two other people that worked there, Chaz and Ray. Ray was a black guy who cooked on the grill. He had been in Vietnam and had that certain grit. He always helped me when I needed it and made me lunch when I came in from school. Chaz was a young white guy who made the subs and was there part time. He was taking a few classes too, but I don't think he was serious about school. He was funny though, because he was a big fan of Elvis and he would talk just like The King. Chaz would grease his hair back and pucker one side of his upper lip sometimes. He was difficult to take seriously, but amusing.

Both Chaz and Tad, who was married, had come on to me. Tad was subtle because he was not in a position to be with another woman, and I certainly was not interested. I was able to stay friendly with both of them.

Chaz and I would go out and party in College Park. Sometimes he would come over to my house and we would drink or get high. He passed out there one night, which was not the first time, as often he would be too hammered to drive. The next morning there was a visitor at the door. It was Ben. Not that it was any of his business, but I did explain to him that I had a friend over, which was the truth. He started crying and wanted to talk.

I'm not sure why, but I told him to give me some time to have my friend leave and then we could talk. It's odd, but I think because

I saw Ben crying it showed a side to him that I thought never existed. I suppose I yearned to see that sensitive side of a man. We talked, and for some crazy, unknown reason, I gave him another chance. So, Ben and I were dating again. Possibly, in the back of my mind, I thought that this was love. In a demented way, I believed that Ben's chasing after me was true adoration. Why else would anyone go to such lengths?

My landlord, John, was jealous of Ben. He would make comments to me about him and say, "Ben seems like a real jerk. You could do better than him." Occasionally, John asked me to go out with him. When I would decline, he would get moody. When I would be in my room studying, sometimes he would open my door without knocking and I would ask him not to invade my privacy. He would get upset. Tension in the house was building.

My roommate, Shelly, was not there much because she often stayed at her boyfriend's house. When she was home, I consulted with her about how I should handle John. She had her boyfriend over that night and invited John and me to join them in their room to party. So we did. We had some beers and Shelly and her boyfriend had coke.

That night helped ease the stress, but there was an expectation from John that we were all buddy-buddy afterward. The fact that John was handicapped made it awkward for me because I didn't want him to think that I was rejecting him because of his disability. I was asking him to respect my space and he was not doing so.

Meanwhile, Ben and his immaturity were wearing on me. At the beginning of us hooking up again, he was driving out to me a lot and buying dinner and drinks when we would go out. But that treatment was short lived. Soon, he wanted me to drive an hour to his house, or to pay a lot when we went out. I wasn't willing to go to those lengths anymore. I tried to break it off again, but he was relentless. This was another dysfunctional relationship with a male in my life that would be like a rubber band stretching back and forth.

Things had also gotten so bad at the townhouse with John that I decided to move. John was not happy and started getting hostile. He would provoke arguments and tell me how well he tended to me by letting me stay there for such low rent. This confused me as I just remember him telling me how much the monthly payment was and that's what I agreed to pay. He would also leave leftovers in the fridge and tell me to help myself, which I never had the desire to do. John would say things like, "You will never find anyone that could treat you as well as me!" It seemed that he was hurt that I was leaving. I remember having a dream about pushing John down the staircase. It scared me.

So I had Ben and John to contend with while I tried to succeed in school. The University of Maryland was demanding and school was still high on my priority list. But I was continuing to get irritated with the university. My paperwork for grants and loans did not go through smoothly, requirements were higher (understandably), and the workload was more demanding. Silly things like parking miles away from your class buildings made life difficult.

I moved to a house in Bethesda, Maryland, that I shared with a guy named Richard and another guy. Richard was a friend of my brother-in-law. I ended up getting a job in a deli in Bethesda too, just because it made more sense, location-wise.

The stress of the move, dealing with John and Ben, and trying to keep up with school was a lot. I was getting high regularly and my drinking continued. I didn't want Richard to know that I was getting high, so I would try and be sneaky by having the window open, and using air spray, Visine, and mints—the usual tricks.

But Richard knew I was smoking pot in my room and said something. Apparently he liked to partake as well. So we ended up getting high together.

Everybody was friendly at the deli. I wasn't going to make a lot of money there, but the hours were convenient and the work was easy. Some of us would go out to the bars in Bethesda after work. One of the managers, Joe, and I became good friends. It was a non-threatening relationship because he had a girlfriend and Ben was still somewhat in my life.

Meanwhile, Scott and I would still go out every now and then. One night we had gone to a bar and had a few drinks inside. We had some coke and pot and wanted to go outside to do some in the car. Little did we know that undercover cops were watching the parking lot at the time. We were under surveillance.

As soon as we got everything out and started using, there was a knock on the window. Scott rolled down his window. We were asked to "step out of the vehicle slowly with our hands in the air." This was not going to be good.

We were informed that the area was under surveillance for the exact reason that we were busted. We were searched and questioned. The police officer wasn't too unfriendly, as cops go. He told us that we would be taken to the police station for processing and the car would be impounded. Scott was upset. He had just gotten the car. Up until then, he had taken the bus and metro everywhere. The policeman told Scott he probably would not get his car back. I felt horrible.

Scott had hidden most of the drugs in a tape case in the console, which the officer didn't find in his initial search. The evidence was what they had on videotape, and paraphernalia. It was the usual fingerprinting, mug shot, and then we had to be bailed out.

Scott told the police he wanted to get some things out of the car before it was taken away from him for good. Somehow the police allowed us to go back to the impound yard and Scott grabbed some things out of his car that he saw for the last time. Some of those things that he grabbed were the drugs he had hidden earlier that the cops never found.

We went to a hotel and got high. But it was difficult to avoid the feeling we both had about the incident. It was obvious that both of us would face charges in court. There would be money put out for lawyers. My family would be so disappointed. Scott had lost his car that he had saved money for and it was partially my fault. The drugs and booze couldn't numb it out that night.

When I got into work at the deli I talked to Joe about the incident. He recommended a lawyer and offered to do whatever he could to help. It meant a lot to me because he didn't seem to want anything from me. I felt like I had a real friend. He was a sincerely nice guy.

I ended up with charges that would be dropped if I went through a program called TASC. I don't even remember what that stands for. I was ordered to go and seek alcohol counseling from a court-appointed individual to determine if I had a problem or not. I was also ordered to go to a facility three times per week where I had to give a urinalysis in front of a person. Then it was tested it to make sure I was clean.

Staying clean was hard for me; I couldn't do it. I would get to the facility and say that I couldn't urinate. So they would give me a cup of water to drink and we would wait. Or they would just consider it positive drug urine. Or, sometimes I would party over the weekend and try and take special herbs that would supposedly get the drugs out of my system quickly. It didn't work. Luckily, I made it through the six months of the program by the skin of my teeth.

I still had a problem, but I had no intention of getting help. Yes, it caused inconveniences here and there, dragged me down a bit at times and the hangovers were a real bitch. The blackouts also worsened to the point that there were times when I really wouldn't remember what I had done the previous night. But maybe that was good. I don't know.

TWENTY

Aside from my on and off again relationship with Ben, my crowd at the time was the people whom I worked with at the deli. Joe and I were becoming pretty close. He had a pleasing character, which was something I was not accustomed to. I started liking him and the feeling seemed mutual.

Joe was also not in the best relationship. He would talk to me about things, and before long we were deep in conversation. It just seemed natural that we should get together, but neither one of us acted on it for a long time. We both had to be out of our relationships.

So I broke up with Ben for the final time and Joe broke up with his girlfriend. Neither one of them took it well.

The inevitable phone calls from Ben came. So did the begging, and the promises of how things would be different. I knew they wouldn't. I was so done with him. And I suppose the possibility of the potential for another relationship helped.

Joe and I did get together. I remember our first kiss. It was spontaneous. We had been to our regular bar that the bunch of us would all go to, Dunmores. At closing time, I was getting ready to go home and Joe was walking me to my car. We chatted for a bit, said "good bye," and he leaned over to give me a kiss. It was sweet.

We instantly became inseparable. Not only did we see each other at work all the time, he also stayed with me at my house. We would sleep together in my twin size bed. It didn't matter where we slumbered; we just wanted to be together. Funny, because Ben was still calling me, even when he knew I was with someone else. Sometimes I would have Joe answer the phone, but it didn't help.

Ben called for a good six to nine months. He would often be drunk and sometimes he would be crying. It was pathetic.

One night, Joe and I went to a party together. His ex was there which didn't matter to me, but it did matter to her. She was inflamed. They fought and she scratched his face.

The next day, I took Joe to meet my mother and her partner at their house in Georgetown. Mom knew that I was quite enamored with him and that we were seriously talking about a future together. My mothers' first impression of Joe was with a huge scratch across his face. It was not positive. I had to explain it as best I could. But the story didn't sound good no matter how rosy I tried to make it seem.

Joe and I were engaged within three months. We had moved into a small apartment in Rockville. I had my two kitties, Chelsea and Sylvester, who had been with me through some tough times already.

When Joe presented me with the diamond engagement ring in that apartment, I ran into the kitchen and crouched on the floor in a corner. I was inundated with so many emotions. I was fearful, flushed and conflicted, but also still an addict and alcoholic. There was a voice inside telling me that I was not worthy of someone asking me for my hand in marriage.

I also remember Joe asking my father for my hand in marriage. We had gone over to my father's house together and Joe was nervous, but he wanted to be proper and do the right thing. My father was living alone in a house in Bethesda at the time. When Joe presented the statement to him, "I would like to have your daughter's hand in marriage." My fathers' response was," Well, I certainly hope you can live with her because I sure couldn't." And then there was an awkward laughter. My father was actually being serious. But I don't think Joe knew. I wanted to die.

The "honeymoon" part of our relationship was short lived, even before we married. We both had tempers and stubborn personalities. Each of us had different ways of coping with the stress of living together and planning a future. We were emotionally young and had bad habits, but cared for each other deeply. Our coping mechanisms at the time were extremely limited and we stood no chance.

Joe and I first bonded because we both liked to party. He was more into booze, I was more into drugs, but I drank and he indulged in the drugs. He also had a gambling habit. Joe liked to bet on college football and basketball. Sometimes, he would bet on the pro games too. When he would win, life was grand. When he would lose, it was terrible. It was the same with my drugs. When I could get them, life was heaven. When I couldn't, it was hell. In our sick minds, I suppose unconsciously it all evened out. It was how we existed.

Joe and I were married on June 4, 1988, by Father Bill, who was his godfather. Father Bill had found Joe in an orphanage when he was an infant and told his adopted parents about him. They already had two older children who were also adopted. According to Joe, he had a wonderful childhood. The thing that struck me about him was that he had a lot of friends and all of them were from his younger years in school. He was lucky.

When Joe and I went on our honeymoon, we chose a place where he could do some gambling. That was fine with me. We went to Orlando for a few days to spend some time in Disney World, which was the more innocent stretch of our trip, and then we went to Nassau in the Bahamas. We stayed in a resort with a casino. There were big screen TVs in the bars where he could watch the football games. I wasn't that interested, but we were in an exotic place and we were together. We spent time on the beach and went snorkeling. It really was gorgeous, though I did not find the natives to be especially friendly.

I had not been to a beach in a long time. The water reminded me of Greece! It was the same transparent, aqua color like the

Mediterranean. Being near such a beautiful shore evoked many memories of the islands where I grew up.

Mr. and Mrs. Scarnecchia June 4, 1988.

When Joe and I went to check out of the hotel we tried using a new American Express card that I had received a month or two prior to our nuptials. But because it was new, I was not supposed to charge a large sum of money on it, so we couldn't use the card. Since Joe had spent all of our cash in the casino, we were stuck on the island. Joe ended up calling the parents of a friend and had them wire us money. They were like second parents to Joe and happy to help. It was an interesting way to start our marriage.

Joe and I moved from the apartment to a townhouse that he owned long before we were together. It was thirty minutes outside of DC. Two of his friends ended up living there with us as well, which initially seemed fun, but eventually this strained our relationship. Of course all of us liked to party. But it was not an ideal situation, considering that Joe and I had just married yet we were living with two other men. I sometimes felt violated. At one point, my panties started disappearing. I found them weeks later sticking out of a roommate's mattress, along with Playboy magazines. I was repulsed. I asked Joe to please confront his friend about the situation. He could not and would not. It was uncomfortable. There were also times when Joe would stay out with "the guys" and he didn't care how I felt. We would fight.

My drug habit was all-consuming. If I didn't have pot or coke, I was thinking about scoring some. I had become fiendish. I would always "take out" a little bit for me to have for later. So, when Joe or friends thought we had run out, I always had a little stash. It was selfish, but the thought of going without was unbearable.

I made the HUGE mistake of quitting school. I'm not sure why. I felt swallowed up by it all—working, getting married, and my lifestyle. What a disastrous blunder to lose sight of my success and aspirations. For a while I was feeling overwhelmed with the classes, but that was no excuse. School should have been a priority and it wasn't. Not moving forward with my education at that point would prove to be a grave mistake.

Now that I had dropped out of school, I had student loan debt to go along with a mortgage, credit card bills, our partying habits and the gambling. But we lived in the moment and there were good moments along with the disturbing and volatile times.

I did broach the subject of children with Joe and he seemed unsure as to whether he or we were ready. I had always wanted children, so it just seemed like the natural thing to do. Meanwhile, I had gone from working in the deli to a high-class salon where the local hoity toity women would come. Joe had gotten me the job there through a friend. I worked for three French hair designers. They were all temperamental and each had his own way of how things should be done. I was the receptionist and I made the appointments for the clients, who were extremely demanding.

It was too hard to please the designers and the clients, all of whom commanded immediate attention. I learned a lot about wealthy people and some of the DC celebrities. Many of them were disliked because they just didn't know how to treat people. In their world, money and prestige were everything. I lasted about eight months.

I had a friend who worked in a residential facility for troubled teens, something I was interested in. She encouraged me to apply for a job there. It was the old "Dad's friend who was in the CIA" connection. Her dad knew my dad. Then later she had been the only one I knew at Woodward High.

So I applied and waited patiently. I was excited and nervous because I really wanted the job. I had never really wanted a job like that before. I would be doing something that I actually desired to do. Also, the money was good compared to what I had been making, and I would have benefits.

I knew I could reach these kids. When you have been through a lot of what they have been through, they sense that. Of course, I couldn't put that on my resume, but when my eventual major ended up being Psychology, helping people was the idea. It was perfect for me.

When the woman from the Human Resource office called to tell me that I had the job, she could tell that I was thrilled. I cheered into the phone.

So I started doing shift work at The Adolescent Center. I loved it. The people were wonderful and they genuinely cared for the kids.

There was training involved. When the students would get out of control, and often they did, it was our job as staff members to intervene. We were first taught how to talk the students down during a crisis. If they were having a tough time with a family issue or angry with a peer, then we would counsel them. This did not always work.

The kids had been sent to The Adolescent Center either through the court system or they had blown it in the school system. In other words, they had been suspended numerous times for various offenses or expelled. Almost all the students had family issues that were sad to read about in their charts. Many of them had drug-using parents and had been abused physically, emotionally, sexually, or all of the above. The idea was for the students to live there during the week and go home on the weekends. Some students did not go home on the weekends; either their parents didn't come and get them or they were court ordered to remain.

The Adolescent Center was not a locked facility so often the students would go AWOL and we would call the authorities. They would either come back to us or be sent somewhere else. Whenever the students entered the facility for any reason, they were to be searched for drugs, paraphernalia, or weapons.

Frequently the students would get upset with each other, things would escalate quickly and we had to physically intervene. This meant escorting them away from one area to another, possibly putting them in a quiet room, restraining them, or using the last intervention, the safety coat. Some of these methods took a little getting used to as they seemed barbaric. But this facility was not a hospital, so we did not have the option to medicate the students. When they got to that emotional place, they were often deemed a danger to themselves or others.

Sometimes the students would get into fights with each other or they would threaten staff and throw things. All of the furniture was purposefully large, heavy, plastic, and too big for them to throw. They still tried. At times they would barricade themselves in their rooms or behind their mattresses and throw things at staff. This is how they released their anger. We would call for support staff from other units to keep situations safe. It was also important for us to document each event.

I worked on a unit with eight middle-school boys. The usual shift was 2:30-11:00 p.m. At times, I would be there for the early shift, which was 7:00 a.m. to 3:30 p.m. We would be there when the boys would come down from school, which was in a separate building. We would have a short meeting to go over their day and then lay out their evening. Often there would be activities planned and, of course, there was dinner. We usually had a more formal unit meeting in the evening for the boys to talk about issues going on with them or each other.

The boys had individual and family therapy that they would go to. Ironically, one of the therapists that worked there was Ann Boyd who had counseled me at Shepherd Place twelve years earlier. She didn't even recognize me.

Working at The Adolescent Center was extremely gratifying. I grew attached to the kids and the hours were fine. I also bonded with other workers. We would all go out after work and party together.

The work was stressful. As co-workers, we relied on each other immensely. There were some people that seemed to be what we called "lifers." These people had gained authority and had been able to work their schedule to make it comfortable for themselves. Sometimes, they did not treat the students well. It was hard to watch. I suppose it struck a sensitive chord in me, as I knew what it was like to be treated in such a way—o not be heard, understood or respected.

It was a bit surreal being there as an employee, especially with my past. I had been on the other side. But here I was in a position to really help some people. Still, in the back of my mind I always knew that I still had this problem that wasn't being addressed. My addiction and alcoholism would cause difficulties occasionally, but at that point I was a "functional" alcoholic and addict.

Joe and I did our usual going out to the bars and getting high. We liked to smoke pot, drink, and do coke. It all went together. I also accepted his gambling.

We would get coke from a friend of Joe's who worked downtown. Normally, we would drive down to the city; get the white, head back home, and party all night. Often, I waited in the car while Joe went inside the building to "score." I would sit, waiting, late at night, in the middle of the city. I would see rats rummaging through the large trash bins, squirming around with their wiry tails. I felt just as filthy as those rodents as time passed in that alleyway.

When Joe would go out with his friends, sometimes he wouldn't make it home. He would end up passing out somewhere. Though he didn't see a problem, it got hard for me to trust him when he wouldn't come home. At times we would have plans only for him to break them, come home hours later, and pass out. I would be angry and would want to talk, but it was hard to talk with a person who was passed out. I would try and bring him to, but to no avail. At times, I got physical because I would be so frustrated and incensed with him. I didn't know any other way to cope with my feelings of despair. The physical abuse I had experienced in an earlier relationship had emerged and was jolted whenever I felt rejected by Joe. He hurt me in a different sort of way; he would ignore me, withdraw, or leave. He was extremely passive-aggressive. He didn't have to say a word but would still be cruel. I didn't know how to deal with him. It was uncharted territory. At the time, I was not willing to look at my own behavior and the effect it had on him.

Joe and I did get into some nasty quarrels. One night, we had been downtown in DC drinking in a bar with friends. I became upset with him as he was flirting with a girl that was with us. Joe laughed it off. As we went outside and the alcohol took full effect, we became embroiled with each other. Joe ended up taking a taxi and leaving me downtown. When I got home, I was furious! He was passed out and I wanted him to apologize. He kept laughing at me instead. This must have been a way for him to manage. I felt deluged with rage. I impulsively grabbed a bottle of pills in the medicine cabinet and swallowed all of them. Joe went to call 911 and I told him not to, I wanted him to see me get sick or hurt. He grabbed the phone and called. When the paramedics came, Joe belittled me in front of them. The ambulance drove me to the emergency room. I had to have my stomach pumped at the hospital. The doctors jammed a tube down my nose to remove everything from my belly. I then had to orally ingest charcoal to absorb the toxins. I had overdosed on pills that eventually would have made my heart stop. It was an episode that gave me pause, for multiple reasons.

As I became more established in my job, it seemed that Joe was becoming antsy in his. He had been a manager at the deli for years and it wasn't going to amount to much. He had worked hard. He had attended the University of Maryland for one or two semesters when he was younger, but college didn't seem to be his thing.

While Joe was still working at the deli, we decided to move into a nice home (townhouse) and sell the one we were living in. A friend of Joe's, who was a real estate agent, lined up places for us to see. We found an adequately-sized townhouse in a more rural area. We thought the location was beautiful because it was untouched country at the time, yet we were somewhat near family, friends, and the city. We were definitely thinking about the future.

The drive was not far from my work, but it was a bit longer for Joe. Most of the furniture we had was from Joe's inheritance when his parents had passed years earlier. It was masculine, but it worked. Basically, all we had were the bare necessities.

I planted a pretty garden out front to make it feel more like home. It was something I had never done. At first I got fanatical with it and Joe helped. Initially, we had to pull out three big bushes that were there and looked hideous. We then put some smaller bushes and decorative grasses to spruce it up. I planted a lovely lilac bush that would send a heavenly scent in to the house every spring. Then I put in coral bells, bleeding hearts, daisies, marigolds, and petunias.

It looked gorgeous. I had pots of geraniums on the steps that bestowed a feeling of nostalgia; they reminded me of Greece. They bloomed all summer long.

We got to know several of the neighbors, and of course we latched on to the ones who liked to get high and drink. There was a couple on each side of us that had been friends already and they would get together regularly. I was a bit wary of the two women because they were best friends. I definitely seemed to have my guard up with women as a result of my past experiences. It just seemed natural.

One couple had several children and the other couple had a newborn that was just adorable. It made me want a child even more.

Joe and I discussed starting a family and we both agreed a year after moving into the townhouse in Gaithersburg. I was ecstatic with the idea of trying to have a child. Despite our issues, in my mind, it would all work itself out.

It did not take long for me to get pregnant. I was thrilled. Joe was petrified. Intellectually, I knew it was important for me to stay off of drugs and booze while I was carrying a child. Before I got pregnant, I was getting high every day, several times a day, as was Joe. We would drink and partake in other substances on the weekends, for the most part.

I pretty much went cold turkey. Once or twice I took a toke off a joint. There were times when I would have a glass or two of wine. Actually, I remember when we were at an award ceremony for my father where he received a medal for his service to the Agency. I had a glass of wine and a woman said something to me about drinking. It felt horrible. My OB/GYN had told me that indulging every now and then was not going to be harmful. But because I did not feel well without having alcohol or drugs, it was not okay for me to rationalize.

On New Year's Eve of 1991, Joe and I were going to spend the evening together. He was going to go out with some friends first to party. I was okay with that. As the evening wore on, and it got later and later, I wondered where Joe was.

He called close to midnight and told me he wasn't coming home. Joe was having too much fun at the bar with Richard. At the time, Richard was living with Patty and I wondered where she was. I called her. She was just as devastated as I was. It was New Year's Eve! I was pregnant! What was he thinking? The sadness and emptiness was more than I could bear. I had Patty to talk to on the phone. It seems she felt pity for me knowing that I was pregnant. Joe did eventually come home and basically just passed out. God damn it!

As time went by, I was crumbling to pieces. I was going through withdrawal from the substances and hormones were kicking in. Joe couldn't handle it. I wanted him there for me and he wanted to be out drinking and carousing with friends. We fought terribly. I felt abandoned. The conflicted emotions inside me were too much to endure. I was not well. Joe moved out.

TWENTY ONE

This was a dismal time in my life. Joe was leaving and I couldn't drink or drug anymore. But he could and he had every intention of partaking. He was apprehensive of all the uncertainties that went along with having a baby.

I had numerous friends at work and they were supportive. My family was there for me. I was ecstatic about the baby, but it was devastating not having Joe.

He did eventually come back. It was like we were friends making up. I loved Joe dearly and wanted him in the baby's life and mine. We took child-birthing classes together. We got the baby's room ready. Joe put up wallpaper that had lambs and chicks. We picked out furniture. He came to the sonogram where you could see the baby's heart beat and we found out we were having a boy. Both of us were blissful! I wouldn't even know what to do with a girl. A boy sounded easier and I secretly wanted a boy. We got some books with lists that went on and on, and picked out a name.

All of this made it more real for Joe and he started trying to ground himself a bit in preparation. Our friends and family had a baby shower for us. I had always been so thin, it was awkward being pregnant, and the emotional roller coaster was unbearable at times. It didn't matter. I wanted this baby.

I passed my delivery date, so my doctor set a date for me to be dilated. We went in to Shady Grove Hospital at 6:30 a.m. in June 1991. When we arrived, there was a wait because, sadly, a woman had just delivered a stillbirth. They put us in a sound free room. They hooked me up to the IV and monitors to keep an eye on my contractions and the baby's heart. I was given Pitocin to get me to start dilating. It did not begin right away. Joe was tired, and distracted by "The Andy Griffith Show" on the TV screen.

My contractions began. They weren't bad for a while, but as they worsened you could see the waves on the monitor. Occasionally, I would moan. At one point, I let out a large groan and Joe looked at the monitor and said, "That one didn't look too bad." I wanted to clobber him.

I made it about ten hours before they gave me an epidural. It still took me a while to become fully dilated. All in all, I was in labor for sixteen hours. I pushed, but really couldn't feel much. Joe watched and seemed amazed when the baby was finally born—a healthy, seven-pound, fourteen-ounce boy.

My mother and her companion Miranda had been out in the waiting room and decided it was okay to just barge in. I was too exhausted and excited to care or say anything. As the nurses were cleaning him, he let out a deep cry. When they put Tony in my arms, he immediately looked up. We bonded instantly. They say that newborns aren't able to see well for the first few days but I know he was looking directly into my eyes.

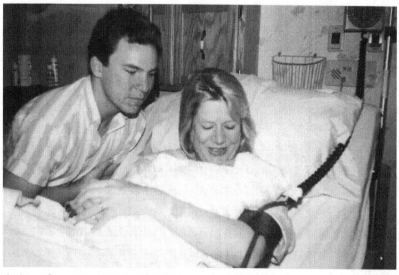

Anthony Scarnecchia born June 1991.

All the worries, fears, wonders, and emptiness were gone the moment I laid eyes on him. He was the most beautiful, perfect baby I had ever seen. He seemed to bring such purity into my heart at that moment. Tony was my life now. I loved him more than life itself forever, unconditionally. I was a mother.

Insurance companies had just changed their policies then, and women who had just given birth were sent home after one night and then a nurse would come to the home and visit. At the hospital, I had a difficult time urinating and kept telling the nurses, but I was sent home and still having a tough time.

I was not feeling well due to a vaginal tear during the childbirth and needing stitches. The nurse had come to visit and I reported my problem urinating. She said I looked awfully swollen which was normal for a lot of women. After a quick check, she said I needed to be catheterized. Joe drove to the hospital to get a kit to do this, and the visiting nurse ended up emptying an astronomical amount of urine from my bladder. Apparently if too much builds up it can become toxic to your system. I had a catheter for a few days and she came back to check on me again.

Settling in with Tony was heaven. He was a charming baby. I breastfed him for a short while, despite my apprehension. He slept in a little bassinet next to the bed and I could just pull him into my arms at night when he needed to be fed.

I would take him for walks in the stroller through the neighborhood. A lovely path ran down to a little pond with cattails, tall grass, and frogs that would croak. Joe was bloated with pride as a father, but there was little he could do with a young infant except hold him and change his diaper. My family embraced this first young prince. Until then, there had only been girls in the family.

Even the cats loved Tony. Joe and I had been told that cats could be envious when you bring an infant home, but we never had a second thought once we saw how the felines adored him. Chelsea would sometimes go into his crib and lie beside him as she purred away.

Tony had bright, blonde hair like I did when I was a child, a little towhead. He was gentle, and easy to please. He looked like an angel when he slept and every moment he was awake was a delight.

Joe and I loved putting adorable outfits on Tony and visiting friends or family. We swallowed up every little milestone that came along. When he would start to smile or giggle, it was such a thrill. Tony was a happy, serene baby. I dreaded taking him to the pediatrician because usually they would have to give him a shot or draw blood. It pained me to know what was coming to my precious Tony and then to see him cry.

It was hard to leave Tony and return to work after six weeks of maternity leave. I wanted to be with him. Most of my shifts were 2:30 to 11:00 at night. Joe and I were able to work our schedules so that we only had someone other than ourselves with him a few days a week. That was crucial.

My old friend Richard, whom I had first lived with in Bethesda, had married Patty. We were all friends. She loved Tony and practically begged to watch him a few days a week for us. She was a godsend. I would drive Tony to Richard and Patty's house about thirty minutes away and then twenty minutes to work. Usually Joe would pick Tony up whenever he would get off. It worked well for us.

Life was good for a while. We were a little family. We appeared to be a normal husband and wife with a darling new baby.

But the drugs and booze called.

I stopped breast-feeding and started partying again. My mind and body needed to get high. The thought of it consumed me constantly. I was an addict and alcoholic.

Despite my addictions, I took care of my new baby boy and I went to work. Life went on. Things were not the greatest between me and my husband. We had tried counseling for the sake of the marriage and our new child. It was difficult for Joe to look at issues. We had many.

Money issues, substance abuse, I was insecure, he was passive-aggressive, the list went on. But Joe felt that I was the one with all the problems, and that he didn't have any. Maybe I was from Venus and he was from Mars. I certainly wore my emotions on my sleeve. It was hard to escape the jam we were in.

Meanwhile, the partying continued. Our little circle consisted of some of the neighbors, friends from my work, Richard and Patty, and a few regulars named Paul and Dean. Every now and then we would throw a big party. A lot of friends liked to come since we had a pool table and dartboard. I always thought I got better at darts the more I had to drink. I didn't.

I would read to Tony first and put him to sleep. He liked it when I held him in the rocking chair. The chair was a shower gift from my sisters. There was a monitor in his room for me to hear him if he stirred. If he woke up, I would go up to his room and tend to him.

Our parties would get wild. One night, when I pushed Joe playfully, he went right through a screen door. Everyone thought it looked hysterical. I guess I didn't realize the screen was there. We would stay up all night drinking, smoking, and snorting. There was always a nuclear group of us that got together regularly as we could predict what the others wanted to do—booze, coke, and weed. Come Thursday or Friday, we were in sync with each other; the urge was strong. Usually, we were well-stocked for at least one evening. The anticipation leading up to scoring the booze, weed, and cocaine was almost as exciting as doing it. It was always frustrating if we couldn't find a dealer or if he didn't have enough for the evening. Sometimes, we would get an eight ball of coke or more for three or four of us and always run out! A quarter ounce was not enough if more people came over than expected to party. There was never enough. This was always the dilemma.

We would need to make a run for more beer and argue over who would venture out onto the road already wired out. Two of us would bravely make the drive together. Surprisingly, we never got pulled over by the cops and never hurt ourselves or someone else on the road. I say this with deep gratitude and shame.

As we would party into the evening, listen to music, talk about nothing, smoke massive amounts of cigarettes, and play darts, I would always obsess about running out. As a dastardly addict, I stashed an extra beer or a few lines, some buds away for myself somewhere. I had to have drugs stored away to get high on, always. But it was inevitable that we ran out and had to come down. While the evenings wore on, and we had already done our extra booze run and possibly gotten more coke, the cigarettes would vanish as well. We would chain smoke as we indulged. Joe and I would reach into the ashtrays and re-light some of the butts; we were so desperate to have the nicotine. The thought is disgusting, but at the time it was a relief to have something to suck on as we hammered the night away. Funny, I would even go through the trashcan and look for long-stemmed butts, and put some of the finer ones aside to smoke.

My addictions picked up right where I left off before I got pregnant. But now I was responsible for a young, heavenly, innocent child. I also had the guilt that weighed on my mind—the sinful thoughts of a lifestyle that served me no more.

Many mornings, I woke up with that appalling feeling of wanting to stop. I would be ill and puking. I would be weary in my heart and sick in my mind. Never again, I would say, never again. But I couldn't stop. I had no control over my own body or mental capacities. The drugs and booze controlled everything.

It wasn't fun anymore. The marriage was in trouble, but I certainly didn't know how to fix it. Maybe if I drank enough or did enough drugs it would all go away?

The writing was on the wall. We literally had sheets hanging from our windows as curtains. We only had bare essentials for décor. All of our money went to our unhealthy lifestyle, and now we had a child to tend to.

Unexpectedly, I became pregnant again! Joe and I were ecstatic with the news.

The beginning of the pregnancy was tough. I was sick. I felt nauseous and was throwing up a lot. Still, Joe and I went on vacation to the beach with my family and actually had a great time.

Once again, the emotional upheaval and disagreements with Joe began.

"Please," I would ask, "can we think about getting help for our drinking and drugging?"

Joe didn't want to and did not let up at that point either.

Joe left me during my second pregnancy. He didn't know when he was coming back. He did not leave because of the baby. Again, he left because he wanted to party and I couldn't. He left because I was in ruins. Once more, it was a hollow time. My heart was shattered.

I had to drum up the strength to be a good mother to Tony. He was my little cherub that I loved so much, and now I had another one on the way. In some ways, having Tony there was my saving grace. I had so much love for this child that I was willing to go on for him, to be strong for him. He was such a ray of sunshine in my life. I worried and wondered if I had enough love for another child. It became just Tony and me. It was the two of us versus the world.

My second pregnancy was different from my first. I was sick a lot, which made it harder. I continued to work at The Adolescent Center About six or seven months into my pregnancy, I had an incident with one of the students on my unit. It was a Sunday night, after they had come back from their weekend passes. One particular student, Stephen, was in a precarious place emotionally from the stay with his family. We didn't know why yet. We had checked his belongings and he went down to his room. His was at the end of the hallway.

I went to check on Stephen. He had thrown his things everywhere around in his room. I told him he needed to put them away. The response was, "Fuck you!" I told him, "I hope you can calm down at some point and talk about what is going on, but you have a level drop for verbal abuse." (A level drop was one of the consequences at The Adolescent Center; they were on a reward system.). Stephen proceeded to attack me verbally again, which I initially ignored. Then he started throwing his belongings at me.

When the items were flying, I put my arm up to protect my face. Then I was backing out of the room and tripped on some of his clothes. I fell. Stephen kicked me in the stomach.

Oh my God, I thought. My baby! My baby!

I was alone on the unit. I screamed for help. Within minutes, two or three people came running down the hall. They probably left their units unsupervised, but I'm sure they could hear the alarm in my voice.

I was hysterical. Stephen was still screaming obscenities at me, as I was walking away from his room. He was oblivious to what he had done. He was out of control. More staff had arrived. Stephen was throwing things at them too and screaming at everyone. He was restrained and safety-coated.

I was taken into the office and consoled. I worried that my unborn child had been harmed. I was driven to the emergency room. They checked me in rather quickly. There was chaos, which I suppose is to be expected. They took blood tests and gave me blankets.

While I lay there desperately trying to hold back tears, a priest came into my room. I was horror-stricken. Why on earth was there a priest there to see me? It was like being visited by the grim reaper.

The priest told me that there had been a young boy who drowned in a pool and did not survive. That was why he was there.

The little boy who had passed was the same age as Tony. I was overwhelmed with grief for the parents of the little boy who died, and for myself. Tears drizzled down my cheeks. The world felt terribly bleak at that moment.

The doctor told me that I had blood in my urine from trauma and that I needed to go to my OB/GYN the next day for an emergency sonogram. He told me that the baby was probably fine. He assured me that they could sustain a lot in the womb.

I went the next day for the sonogram, alone, and my unborn child was fine. It was a traumatic experience. There were so many quiet tears.

TWENTY TWO

Shortly after that incident, Joe did come back. It was hard for him to be away. He loved Tony and me, and he knew that it wasn't right for him to be elsewhere. In his own way, he was upset about what had happened to me at work, but it was difficult for him to comfort me during such situations. Deep down, he too probably was scared that something could have happened to the baby.

I returned to work approximately one week later. Because I was pregnant, I couldn't do any hands on work with the kids, restraints, or safety coatings. Stephen was not there. He had been sent to another facility.

There was a formal meeting with all the administrators from The Adolescent Center and myself. Basically, they were trying to see how I was handling the whole incident emotionally and physically. I sat there with a pink maternity dress on and my round, pregnant tummy sticking out. Swearing to myself that I wouldn't cry during the meeting, I still ended up in tears as I described the incident and the terrifying hospital visit.

The CEO was sorry about what had happened, but glad that I was fine and that my baby was uninjured. All of them seemed grateful that I was back at work.

The rest of my pregnancy was uneventful. Joe's being home helped my state of mind. I would take Tony for his walks on the path when I could, or to the playground. He had little friends that he liked to get together with and favorite toys that he would play with for hours. Tony loved Thomas the Tank Engine. In the summer months I would take him to the baby pool in the neighborhood. He would play so well with the other little children. Tony was a sweet, mild mannered boy.

We took a family trip that summer to the Outer Banks with my dad, his wife, my sisters, and their spouses. My sister Sheila and her husband Bob had two daughters, Heather and Emily, who were adorable! We rented a huge house on the water, which I loved because it always made me think of Greece. The water was clean and warm. The beaches weren't too crowded during the day. In the evenings, we would watch the sun drop down over the ocean with a wonderful breeze constantly blowing. When we were younger as a family, we would go to Ocean City or Fenwick Island. I loved any beach, but I didn't like the crowds.

We had a little pop-up tent to put Tony in when it would get too hot for him during the day. He would nap there. He was always well behaved and we never had a problem. We brought a blow-up raft to fill up with water so that he could soak in his little "Tony pool." It was hard for me to get comfortable with my swollen belly. I tried to lie on a raft, but it just didn't work well. So I dug a hole in the sand for my pregnant stomach and lay on my tummy with comfort. Tony would lie on my back. It was just the two of us. Or, we would sit by the ocean together and just stare out into the water. Just like when I was a little girl, I would gaze out into the waves, wondering what was out there, on the other side. I sat there with Tony and pondered: Do I have enough love for another child?

By the end of the summer, I had gained quite a bit of weight and had gotten hemorrhoids, which were disgusting and uncomfortable. I was constipated, but my doctor told me that all of these symptoms were normal for pregnancy.

I was due in November and worked close to the end. The pregnancy gave me hot flashes and I would try and keep it cool at work. Everyone gave me a hard time jokingly. They understood. There was such a kinship among the people on my unit. I got along with almost everyone at The Adolescent Center, though there were some whose methods I disagreed with and at times we did butt heads.

Joe and I had prepared for the run to the hospital. We knew we were having a boy and one of the names we liked was Devin. Several days after my due date, my water broke one evening and we got ourselves to Shady Grove Hospital.

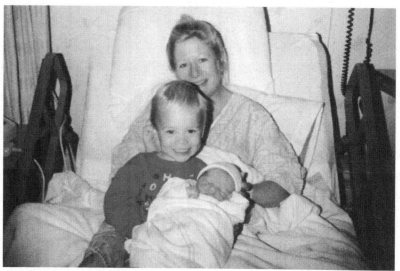

Maxwell Scarnecchia born in November 1993.

Things moved along more rapidly this time. They had redone the labor wing, so I had a beautiful suite with lights and equipment that popped down from the ceiling. It was modern and comfortable.

I asked for the epidural sooner, maybe after six or seven hours. I was dilating quickly and I also remembered the relief I had gotten from the injection the last time. It helped a lot.

Our second son was born in November 1993. He weighed eight and a half pounds. He had a head full of thick, dark hair and was quiet. He was all pureness and gorgeous, just like his brother.

Joe and I immediately decided that he did not look like a Devin. We named him Maxwell Peter. The middle name was after my father since Tony's middle name was after Joe's father, Palmer. I just adored this new baby; I had no more doubt. I instantly loved him with all my heart and soul. God had blessed us a second time.

I had one night to stay in the hospital, as it was the insurance policy. This time I did not have the difficulty with urinating as I did the first time I gave birth. I told the nurses about what happened to me when I was in there two and a half years prior. Amusingly they said, "Oh, we've heard about you!"

When Joe brought him in to see his new brother, Tony looked enormous compared to Max. Tony was quite smitten with his new baby brother. He wanted to hold him. He was gentle and loving. You could see the compassion and curiosity in his eyes. It was a beautiful, memorable sight.

We brought Max home and Joe tended to me for the first day or so. He tried, in his own way. I remember him making me grilled cheese the way I liked it, open face. Tony wanted to be close to the baby; this was his brother. We had the bassinet in the bedroom and I breastfed.

Max was just as perfect as his brother, but different in many ways. From the beginning Max showed his strong will, though he was not a difficult child. He was an angel. But if he didn't want to do something, he made it clear. Max would resist or just not do it.

As with most babies, it took several months for him to finally sleep through the night, which can be an exhausting time for both parents. I was lucky to have the maternity time off as we all gradually grew in to a new pattern and adjusted to our new addition. But he didn't want to nap during the day. I was tired.

My heart ached when I had to return to work and leave my babies behind. Again, Joe and I adjusted our schedules so that Tony and Max were with us as much as possible. We had the boys go with my sister Sheila, as she had offered. Sheila lived north of us and the drive was not easy, especially late at night when I got off work. Truthfully, knowing the boys were in such good hands was reassuring. Sheila took such good care of her own daughters and they all loved Tony and Max dearly. Sheila and her husband Bob lived in a beautiful but simple log cabin that was literally built by hand years earlier.

Joe was now in the lighting design business. He had started out with a company that his old childhood friend had been doing work with. It seemed to be gratifying work for him, but the hours were long and late in to the night. We had discussed my working part-time and we agreed it was a good idea for me to be with Tony and Max.

Working part-time was like having the best of both worlds. I was working at a place where I loved the work, with people I liked. And I was able to be with my new family. My children were young and needed their mother.

⌗

My eventual return to drugs and alcohol was inevitable. I knew the numbers to call to get what I needed and I was right back where I left off. Joe and I would have our ups and downs. We were a married couple with kids and we fought. But things got worse. I was never okay unless I had my drugs or booze. I needed something to take the edge off. In my mind, I took good care of the boys. I was a good mother.

Joe would stay out more either to be with friends or "work." This caused great tension between us. I'll never forget one night when Joe and I were arguing. We were yelling so loudly, it woke Tony and I could hear him in his crib, crying. He called out to us. For me, that was a huge turning point. We were not living harmoniously and my sweet anger Tony, who was a baby, knew this.

One weekend, Joe was going to be gone all weekend for work. According to Joe, he had a gig at the Mayflower Hotel downtown and would be staying there all weekend, rather than driving home in between setting up and taking down the equipment at horrendous hours. Joe said he would be staying there with his partner, Jay. Joe wanted me to get him some foot powder or spray because he had funky smelling feet. I got him both.

When Joe got back from his weekend job, everything seemed normal, whatever that means. A day or so after the weekend I discovered my Mason Pearson brush with long, kinky, blondish strands of hair. There were a lot of them and they weren't mine. I'm sure they weren't Jay's. I already felt insecure about Joe, his usual whereabouts, and his honesty. My heart sunk when I found the brush. I asked Joe about it. He very casually replied, "Oh, Jen stayed with us too. She was on the job."

For that moment in time, I believed Joe. I took his word because I so desperately wanted to think he respected me and that my family really was not falling apart,

Shortly after, Joe and I went to a holiday party given by someone from his company. Of course, we had plenty of coke and there was booze galore. Jen was there with her boyfriend. It was awkward. Several days later, Joe received a gift from Jen and her boyfriend. In my gut, things felt off. I phoned Jen's boyfriend. We spoke for a while. It turned out that Joe and Jen stayed at the Mayflower Hotel alone together. The gift that Joe received was from Jen only. There was more. It was like being stabbed in the heart as I spoke to this man on the phone. He was so hurt too. I knew it was over for Joe and me.

That day when he came home I told him about my talking to Jen's boyfriend on the phone. Joe minimized it, as usual. He said nothing was going on between him and Jen, "nothing physical." I asked Joe to leave. He agreed. I requested that he sign a written financial obligation to the house and the boys. He did.

TWENTY THREE

was frightened. How would I care for the boys? Could I hold on to the house? There were so many questions, so many fears. Joe whistled away as he packed. Then off he went.

I'll never forget the pain, the guttural stabbing that I felt in my womb. As my spouse went off to his independent life, I curled up on the bed that we shared, crying. I was paralyzed by loneliness.

It felt as though Joe had abandoned me and the boys. I called Joe's godfather who was now a bishop, Father Bill, and begged him to speak to Joe. I also hoped that one of Joe's friends would talk some sense into him during this complex time. One of my friends wanted to send some people to put a "hurting" on Joe, but I couldn't allow that to happen to my children's father. For a while, all I could do was wallow in my pain, and to numb out with my drugs and booze.

The boys were my saving grace. Despite my dysfunction, I was able to care for them because I loved my children more than life itself. I read to the boys at night, and gave them baths. They ran through the house giggling. I loved tickling them and hearing their roars of laughter. We would sit out front on the steps and play with bubbles or chalk. The neighborhood kids liked coming to our house.

The first time Joe came to take the boys for a visitation, I felt as though my heart, skin, brain, hair, and fingernails had all been charred and torn from me bit by bit. The emotional turmoil of him taking Tony and Max was almost too much to endure. We would argue and fight. Joe would still do his passive-aggressive bit that would drive me nuts. He wouldn't come on time or inevitably he would bring the boys back late. It got so bad between us that I wasn't sure he would bring Tony and Max back from his visits. I begged my father to speak to Joe and reason with him.

My parents liked Joe. He was actually a personable guy, around others. Mom and Dad decided they could mediate somehow and get Joe and me together to resolve our differences. I was nervous, but I thought my parents should know about this extramarital relationship with Jen.

We gathered in the Bethesda bungalow that Mom was renting at the time. Mom and Dad both mooched a cigarette off of me before Joe arrived. They were definitely stressed. We all sat in the living room. Mom had some little munchies for everyone but no one ate.

Mom started by expressing her concern over Joe's situation and mine. She said that she and Dad wanted to help if they could. The room was very tense and there were multiple moments of what seemed like endless silence. I wanted a cigarette, a drink, anything to help me get through. I decided that I would say something about Joe and Jen. I felt that his being off with this young woman was unacceptable; he was married and had two very young children. I know Mom and Dad cared a great deal for their grandchildren.

Joe then recounted the last seven to eight years of our lives of drug and alcohol use. He went into detail about the wild parties, and us drinking and drugging long into the nights as people went in and out of house. WHAT? I didn't believe what I was hearing. These were tales that I was going to take to my last dying breath; nobody was supposed to know about some of these details—least of all my parents! My feet would not have carried me if I had stood up at that moment. My mind and body were numb.

I don't remember much else from that I evening, but I do recall my father, Mr. CIA, a bigger than life figure to me at the time, the man whose handkerchief I had cried over when I felt so lost as an incarcerated rebellious teenager. He looked at me with a petrifying gaze and said, "Patricia is this true what Joe is telling us?" I immediately responded with, "No Dad, he's lying."

Joe talked about what a great mother I was, but said that I had a drug problem. Of course, Joe could blame it all on me. His family was gone; there was no one for him to be accountable to. My parents wanted to know why Joe had not come to them to get help for me if this indeed had been the case. He had a very difficult time answering this question.

Of course I was a good mother. I was the one that would get up and take care of Tony and Max while he was passed out in bed. Joe was never the one with the problem; it was always everyone or something else.

At the end of the talk that night in Bethesda, my mother looked at me and said, "Patricia, if everything that Joe is telling us is true, I am going to take those kids away from you." I knew she could and would.

⊞

The darkness in my soul at that moment was too much. I could not, would not, lose my babies, my angels. I felt as though I had been flung off a merry-go-round that was going 100 mph. I was so distraught that I could not wrap my head around the moment.

I knew for so long that I had a problem with drugs and booze. I wanted to get help, but could not do it by myself.

Mom wasn't stupid; she knew what she was doing. Mom had a place where I could go, and this became a moment of surrender. Apparently, I had some choice words for Joe or Mom, but I was out of it. I don't remember. During that meeting, Dad lent Joe and me several thousand dollars to get our house out of foreclosure.

This was my bottom: On the verge of a divorce, the house in foreclosure, the threat of losing the boys. I needed to get clean.

I was not willing to go inpatient anywhere. I wanted to be with Tony and Max. Being incarcerated as a teenager played a part in my decision as well. So, I went to Suburban Hospital Outpatient Rehab.

The rehab was right down the street from one of my drug dealers. I would drive by his house on purpose just to test my will power. Not knowing how difficult it was going to be to get clean and sober, I felt determined.

☷

My first day of sobriety was July 10, 1995.

I did the "intense" outpatient program at Suburban. I was at the hospital four days a week and attended mandatory 12-step meetings on the other days. This was my program for about three months. Then I went to "less intense" for another six months. I was at the hospital for one night and meetings several times a week. I did all this for nine months! My counselor, Patty, who was younger than me, looked a bit like Dorothy Hamill. In recovery herself, she was healthy and had spunk. I liked her okay. I dealt with multitudes of counselors, therapists, educators, and nurses at Suburban. I would have to piss in a cup every day so that they could see if I was using or not. The first thirty days my urines were "dirty."

In hindsight, I did not realize what horrible shape I was in. Of course, this was a huge juncture in my life, unbeknownst to me at the time. Basically, I just put one foot in front of the other and let the cards fall as they may. I was in survival mode.

At the time, I probably weighed 95 to 98 pounds. I would get to the hospital, sit down, and try to soak up as much learning as I could. For about two weeks I had the "shakes;" I could not sit still in the sessions at the hospital or meetings. I sweated bullets. My mind would wander. It would race. If I could have peeled off my skin and crawl out, I would have; I was that uncomfortable. I couldn't sleep. My stomach churned constantly, I couldn't eat, and if I did, it wasn't much. Sometimes I vomited after eating. I wanted to punch everybody and anything.

My mind and body were flooded with the newness of getting clean. It was imperative at the time that I learn about detoxing. I was certainly struck to learn about "wet brain" and the alcoholics who ended up in facilities who could not care for themselves. This was a brain disorder, also known as Wernicke-Korsakoff syndrome that comes on suddenly and is often considered to be "alcohol-related dementia," as brain damage can cause difficulties with learning and memory functions that may be permanent and irreversible. Those who end up with this condition end up eventually dying. The thought was frightening. Hearing the chopper land on the hospital roof impacted me as well. That could be ME being flown to the trauma unit! That was a place I never wanted to experience.

Life seemed unbearable, but everyone kept telling me, "It gets better." Other people in recovery were friendly, offering to help in any way or to give me a call if I needed someone to talk to. This sort of camaraderie was foreign to me. What did these people want?

At a sober gathering, I met "Karen." She was getting out of Montgomery General Rehab and needed a place to stay. I told her I was renting out a room in my basement and she could stay with us.

Tony and Max were my salvation. We would play together around the house or go to the park. The boys loved me pushing them on the swing or going down the slide with them. We would go for long walks together on the pathway in our development. I would take them to the mall where they could run around in the children's area. Tony was a social butterfly, always meeting a new boy or girl wherever we were. He was in pre-school at the local high school, which was run by Mrs. Brown. Her pupils were the high school students who would tend to the youngsters. They adored Tony, but Max would miss his brother terribly when he was gone. I dreamed of me and the boys in the future—together, happy and with my misery behind us.

Before Joe and I separated, The Adolescent Center had allowed me to split a position with another person and I was working part-time. Now that I was a single mother, I needed to return as a full-time employee. Unfortunately for me, I was one of the few people working in my department who had children. When I went to the Residential Supervisor to ask if there was any way for me to finagle my schedule so that I could work full-time but be with my boys as much as possible, she was not very accommodating. What I did after that was something I paid for later in a huge way.

I went to the CEO of The Adolescent Center, Mr. Garner. He was a grandfather and dedicated family man. I explained my dilemma and asked him if there was some way I could come back to work full time but still be with my children. He obliged. So, I ended up working two sixteen-hour days a week, going in at 7:00 a.m. and leaving at 11:00 p.m. Mr. Garner's rationale was that the schedule we concocted would be so unappealing to the other staff that nobody else would request the same accommodation. But it was worth it to me to be with Tony and Max. Amazingly I was able to pull this off, but this schedule swallowed up immense amounts of emotional and physical energy.

Another godsend was a wonderful woman I found to take care of the boys in our home, Theresa. She would bring her two children with her to the house. Joe and I worked out our schedules so that Tony and Max were with her only two or three days a week. The boys adored Theresa. She would do arts and crafts with them or take them to the park. I knew that Tony and Max were happy even when Joe or I couldn't be with them, and that was important. During such a tumultuous time, little things, and meaningful people were paramount.

Tony and Max had been with a different caretaker, Tina, for a while in her home before we found Theresa. Tina was nice and had a son. At times, she cared for a few other children from her development as well. There was nothing like the boys running to my arms in sheer joy when I would go to retrieve them after work. We were all so glad to see each other and go home. When I worked late shifts, they would be asleep when I arrived. I would carry them to the car in their pajamas, groggy and trying so hard to decide whether they wanted to stay asleep or wake up.

After some time, I could see that Tony was not happy. He said that Tina would make him eat liver or brussel sprouts, even if he didn't like them. I sat with Tony and we talked about this. He was distressed. Tony would have to sit at the table and finish what was on his plate or go hungry. Tony was such a well-behaved young boy. I couldn't imagine him being disciplined for such a ridiculous rule. I wasn't happy. I called Tina and she confirmed that whatever was served for lunch or dinner is what the children were expected to eat. Those were the rules in her house. Certainly, they were not my rules. And I knew firsthand how rules such as hers had affected me—I grew up with eating problems that I struggled with during various times of my entire life. I always tried to be healthy. As a young girl, I remember having to sit at the table for long periods of time because I would not eat what was on my plate. It clearly became a control issue.

I suppose I also did not want my son subjected to this sort of treatment when Joe and I were paying for him to be cared for in a nurturing environment. I would have been happy to bring food for Tony.

Karen, who I met at Montgomery General when I would go to recovery gatherings, moved in to my basement as a renter. She had relapsed many times before and had a ghastly stack of bills from hospitals and rehabilitation centers that she had been in prior to Montgomery General.

She appeared to be serious about recovery and had a boyfriend, Don, who was supportive of her well-being. Karen had lost temporary custody of her 11-year-old daughter who was living with Karen's ex-husband in West Virginia. She was worried that her ex-husband's stepchildren (adolescent boys) might have been molesting her daughter. If Karen stayed sober for a certain amount of time (six to nine months) she could get her daughter back.

Karen and I went to sober meetings and events together. There was a club near Montgomery General where people gathered to socialize. We met some men there that were quite flirtatious. It felt flattering to have some male attention.

Miles and I seemed to hit it off. Little did I know how out of my mind and vulnerable I was from getting off the drugs and booze. I was advised by my counselor and therapists at Suburban not to make any huge changes in my life, one of those being getting in to a new relationship. It was important for me to stay focused on getting well.

Being stubborn and thick headed, I thought I could handle it. Miles and I became entangled in what we thought was a romantic and loving relationship. He was a recovering junkie with long hair that he wore in a ponytail and he had a thick mustache. Miles labeled himself an ex-biker. Possibly this meant that he had to sell his bike for drugs or got kicked out of a club. He drove a beat up Toyota. When I met him, he was slim and wore jeans, t-shirts, and black leather jackets. He wore a bandana on his head, which looked better over his receding hairline. Miles was broke and earned money doing odd jobs. He had been a drug dealer but was trying to clean up his life. I was thirty-five years old when I got sober and met him. He had been living with friends. Miles and I would go to recovery gatherings, where there were many "low bottom" drunks and addicts. People would smoke in these places, rather clubs, and I would get ill from the cloud-filled rooms despite the fact that I smoked also at the time. Miles's claim to fame was that he had been featured on *America's Most Wanted*, but he was not the actual criminal being highlighted. He happened to be in prison and broke out with someone who was considered to be "armed and dangerous." This should have been a sign to me, but it wasn't.

Miles and I submerged ourselves in a "relationship." I believe that my brokenness drew me to him. The fact that a man was so focused on me was a bit of a confidence booster. He would drop me off at the hospital and take me to work. We would write poetry to each other and long to be in each other's arms.

Miles pressured me to move in, but it didn't take much convincing. I allowed him to, and of course he had already met Tony and Max. He had few belongings and basically they all went in my room and the living room. He had always kept snakes or lizards wherever he was and we decided to get an iguana. Tony was thrilled, considering his love for creatures. There were friends who would roar up to the house on their Harley-Davidsons and many others that would come over for barbecues and hangouts. For a while, there was good clean fun at the house, odd as that sounds. I wasn't sure if I would have fun again when I gave up the booze and drugs.

Pretty much as soon as I got clean, I developed incapacitating migraine headaches. I would get them four to five times a week. I sought out a neurologist and he diagnosed them. There had been breakthroughs in medicine for migraines since I had been an adolescent, one in particular that came in the form of an injection. I would try giving myself the shots of Imitrex. My insurance only covered a certain amount per month. The injection was remarkable for a new user as the needle was embedded in a plastic vessel. I would place it against my leg and push a button.

The first time I used my injection, I was at work. I had been warned about the side effects. I would be extremely dizzy and light headed for about twenty minutes (and may not have been able to function well, the doctor had told me). I would probably need to lie down until the medication took full effect. It was well in to my shift and I had a headache for several hours that was getting worse by the minute. Luckily, it was the day shift and I had the students in the morning. I had prepared them for the day and got them up to the school building. Basically, I was doing paperwork and errands for our unit.

I walked to the bathroom with my injection. It was in a brown paper bag. I pulled my jeans down to my knees. My head was throbbing. Every sound, movement, and blink of my eyes brought more agony. I was slightly apprehensive about the needle, and more so about whether it would work or not. I pulled out the plastic, blue contraption. It lay on my thigh for about thirty seconds until I pushed the button. Kejuk! The needle punctured my flesh and I immediately felt a rush of pain, pressure, and pounding that urged me to get out of the bathroom. My skin began to bubble with sweat and my heart was drumming.

I knew I needed to lie down. I had experience with bathroom floors but felt that at this point in my life I had moved beyond hugging the commode. Quickly, I wrapped everything back into the wrinkled tan bag and went to the privacy of my unit.

All I could think was, "please let me feel some relief!" There was a couch in our staff office. I closed the unit and office doors, turned out the lights and waited as quietly as life would allow.

About ten minutes later, I could hear the unit door open. I tried as best I could to get it together under the circumstances. There I was in darkness sitting on the couch. I think I even had a little blanket. In front of me were standing the CEO, Mr. Garner, and some visiting parents who were touring the facility. I was honest and explained my predicament: This headache, shot, and the need to rest for a few minutes.

Mr. Garner could not have been more empathetic to my situation and state of embarrassment. He actually apologized to me for his intrusiveness. Being very aware of issues that I had been dealing with, Mr. Garner said, "You rest all you need to. Let me know if I can help in any way. I hope you feel better soon."

I was so appreciative for a caring heart and hand. To my great relief, my headache subsided after approximately forty minutes. The shot worked! It was like migraine magic!

Soon, Miles got wind of my injections. According to him, he also got migraines. Again, Miles had been a junkie. No big surprise that he wanted to use my Imitrex when he was "struck" with a migraine.

Miles somehow extracted the needle out of the applicator. He wanted to have full control of what he was injecting. He would put it in his vein, pump some medicine in, and then pull some blood out. He liked "playing" with his blood and the medicine. I have seen other junkies do this as well. It reminded me of drug foreplay, almost like holding off as long as you can to have an orgasm. Miles liked the rush from the Imitrex, it gave him sort of "sensation," despite the fact that it was non-narcotic. This was a turning point for us, the beginning of the end.

I started pulling away from Miles. I felt as though he was taking advantage of me, which he was. He did not have a regular job or home. His car was a piece of shit and he had the nerve to inquire about my medical insurance as a possible benefit for him (he would pretend to be Joe).

Part of the change between the two of us was possibly attributed to the fact that I was getting my wits about me; my mind was clearing. I told Miles that we shouldn't be in a relationship and he was taken aback. He begged for me to reconsider, or to at least "think about it." We did the yo-yo thing for a week or two. He went and stayed with friends for that duration, which I appreciated.

During that time, Miles came to my place of work to "talk to me." The Adolescent Center was a state facility with adolescents residing there. Nobody could just walk on to the premises. He put my job in great jeopardy.

At that point, I decided to have Miles move his belongings out of my home, which he was not happy about. I didn't care! He wavered for weeks and made life uncomfortable for me, but eventually Miles did retrieve his clothes, desk and other miscellaneous items. Before doing so, Miles wanted to have one last conversation. I agreed.

He came to pick me up in his car. We drove to a park not far from my house. It was dusk, and he set the car a bit away from a street lamp. I could see the expressions on his face as he spoke. Miles was quite distraught. His eyes were puffy and dark. The dialogue coming from his mouth was low and strained. I wasn't sure if he was high or not. I knew he had relapsed several times. He definitely was not right and I knew that I had made a bleak mistake by coming.

Miles said in a rigid tone, "You lied to me; you said you loved me, but the poems you wrote are bullshit!"

I replied, "Miles, I'm sorry that you are hurt. I want different things for myself right now, and my feelings for you have changed."

I explained to him that I felt he moved in too soon and that he had taken advantage me, my early recovery, and my vulnerable state of mind.

What ensued at that point was something I never expected.

Miles pulled out a revolver. He never pointed it at me or at himself for that matter. This was a gun that I knew Miles had, but he had kept it at a friend's house. Miles was an ex-con and legally could not be in possession of a firearm. Miles said he did not want to go on if we couldn't be together.

I said, "Miles, you will find someone else. Our timing was not right, and I need to be focused on my sobriety."

Fear inoculated me. I wasn't sure if Miles could see my heart thumping. I knew I needed to stay as calm as possible, despite as panicked as I felt.

How dare he put me through this! I was enraged with Miles in that moment. In my mind, I felt like we had given a relationship a try and it didn't work. Okay, so move the hell on! I was raw with emotions and thoughts at that point in my recovery. I didn't know who I was or what I was feeling.

Miles knew how much my getting clean meant. Tony and Max were more precious to me, but I did not want him to fixate on them, as he seemed unhinged. I couldn't predict what he was going to do at that moment, the next day, or whether I would even make it home that night. I felt as if I were in a twilight bubble, and that one wrong move or word would determine if I made it out or not. Was this really happening?

Miles did agree to think about going it alone, to my relief. He drove me home. I didn't sleep all night. Tony and Max had been sneaking in to my bed at nighttime, which gave me great solace. They were my little tribe.

The next day, I called the police. According to them, I was in a difficult situation, as Miles had not actually threatened me. I felt great frustration with two little boys to protect and being a single mother. This man had a gun, for God's sake!

I changed the locks right away!

Miles slowly disappeared. He stayed with friends for a week or two and then moved away, much to my comfort. I never heard from him or about him after that.

Karen was still living in the basement. She, too, had relapsed and I would find her very tweaked or passed out. Her boyfriend was beside himself about her returning to drugs; he felt that this was her final run with rehab and getting sober. I couldn't let her stay in the house if she was going to continue using.

Once a month, Karen could have supervised visits with her daughter at the county office. She would get so excited and would buy some little treats for her daughter, like candy or a stuffed animal. I took her to one of her "visitations." The building was about thirty minutes from my home. The office was on the third or fourth floor of the county building. Up the elevator we went. The supervisor was waiting and I believe she searched Karen before going in. Karen had one hour with her daughter. One hour. Sixty minutes in a thirty-day period, while someone watched over this poorly flawed mother and her innocent daughter. It was one of the saddest things I had ever witnessed. Her 11-year-old didn't want to leave; she wanted to stay with her Mom. Karen's ex was in another room. I'm not sure why, but possibly due to the animosity between them, they could not be in the same room together. The emotional turmoil that was so apparent that day will never leave my brain or my heart—a mother so far removed from her child due to her addiction and alcoholism. The shame and despair in Karen's eyes and the longing in her child's eyes haunt me. They were so far from each other, even as they embraced. It is weaved in to my soul forever.

Karen tried as best she could to stay off drugs and booze. But for her, it seemed that sobriety was fleeting. The third time she came to my house trashed, she and Don got into a fierce fight. It was late at night when I came home. Karen had locked the top bolt and I was not able to get in (the key, which was a different one, had been long lost). It was total chaos!

July 1995, newly sober and holding Max.

I called Joe and told him that I didn't know when the boys could come home due to the situation. He was perturbed but it was beyond my control.

I did get into the house that night and Karen was near comatose. Don was devastated. He said he had seen her like that twenty or thirty times. In the morning, I told Karen that she could not stay. I felt as though I had given her enough chances. She knew it was coming. I was doing the best I could to get a handle on my own life and could not deal with the additional external stressors that were going on.

Karen packed what few belongings she had at that point. I had given her some clothes. I don't know where she went from there. I stayed in touch for a short while and knew that Karen continued to struggle with staying clean.

Six months after Karen left, I saw her obituary in the local paper. She was thirty-five years old—the same age as me at the time.

TWENTY FOUR

made it through rehab. The places where I sought continued recovery were not to my liking and so I searched for more adequate wellness centers that suited me. Since Tony and Max were so young, and money was tight, I brought them with me. They were well behaved and never a disturbance to anybody.

My family was so supportive of my getting clean. We all went on a trip to the beach the summer of my first year. It was with my Dad, his wife, Sharon, my sisters, and their families. Of course, I brought Tony and Max. On that trip nobody brought wine or beer. Everyone knew how tempting it would be if there was alcohol.

The family adored Tony and Max, especially their cousins, Heather and Emily. We had lived near them and their mother, my sister Sheila, and she had taken care of the boys for a while. So, we had all grown quite close.

When Sheila got married, her husband Bob was extremely religious and she gravitated back to Catholicism. I would go to some of her bible study groups. Spirituality was definitely becoming important to me and I felt it should be something to expose the boys to as well. Tony was asking questions about God and I didn't feel well equipped to answer. As a mother, I needed to cultivate a spiritual life for the boys. I felt it should be a decision we all made together, but I wanted to at least seek out different churches and see where I felt comfortable. Joe and I had never had the boys baptized when they were born. I wondered where I should go to explore this very personal decision.

In lieu of my upbringing, I found myself in Unitarian, Baptist, and Methodist churches, and a Synagogue of Jews who believed in Jesus! The synagogue members were a lively and friendly bunch, and they scooped me up lovingly, always offering free bread to take home if I needed.

Interestingly, I felt uneasy in any place of worship that was not a Catholic Church. I wanted to receive communion, and I wanted to kneel on the pew and pray. So my search for a Catholic Church began. I went to four or five churches. Then I found St. Rose of Lima. The music was uplifting and glorious, not somber. Everyone joyfully sang along.

My call back to God and the church fostered a nurturing environment for the boys and me. We felt right at home at our church and all wanted to go each Sunday. St. Rose was a liberal Catholic church, if there is such a thing. Father Dugan gave an enlivening homily each week. He was saddened by what was going on in the Catholic Church at the time and eventually left.

Tony and Max went through the Catechumen process. They were baptized, received First Holy Communion, and became confirmed.

Tony, Max, and I would go on a retreat in a quiet place in the mountains, where there were few of us but our small community. We learned to pray, be still with our thoughts, and reflect on moments when possibly we could learn to trust God. It was a simple place, where we could appreciate what family meant, the gifts of having food on the table, and a bed to sleep on. The boys were thrilled to be there and remember the experience fondly. We would go for walks in the woods. In the evenings, we would play festive games.

Getting clean was a foreign to me. I would go to sober dances, but I didn't know how to dance without being drunk. My legs felt like large, heavy tree trunks. I was uneasy speaking to people in social settings. What would I say? What would I talk about? As silly as that sounds, it's the truth. I wasn't sure how ready I was for all of it, but I knew I couldn't go back.

I met many wonderful people in recovery. I also put people from the past behind me.

I flung myself into being the best mother possible. Tony, Max, and I were inseparable when I wasn't at work. We did all kinds of joyful things together. Tony loved creatures and collecting ants for his ant farms. Once, he was searching for a queen ant to have his own little colony. We mail ordered red ants, but he found out that their bite is severe. Joe also built a beautiful ant farm as tall as he was for Tony, truly made with love. We would visit the Insect Zoo at the National Museum of Natural History and take many other trips to the city to see the sights.

The boys and I would go to fairs, water parks, museums, the zoo, the park, and the circus with friends and family. We swam in our neighborhood pool in the summertime and found indoor pools in the wintertime. We would go to the beach with my family (Bethany and the Outer Banks). We even discovered a padded playground in the mall for fun on the cold days.

The boys possessed something that I would never have, childhood friends that they grew up with—ties they would cherish forever. The memories of them playing in the woods with ten to twelve other boys and girls are priceless. The yelling and roars of laughter will echo in my heart always. Whether it was cops and robbers or building a fort, Tony and Max had an enchanted young life.

Joe and I tried to keep things as normal as possible for the boys, despite our situation. We would plan fun birthday parties for the boys, inviting all of their friends and our relatives. We did pony rides, Chuck E. Cheese, laser tag at Shadow Land, and the bowling alley. When Joe and I first separated, before we had actually divorced, we had a pony ride in the back yard for Tony's birthday and Joe was flirting with our ex-neighbor. I'm not sure if he was doing it because we weren't together anymore, or this was how he naturally acted. I was thankful to be away from him, but my resentment towards him was still an issue.

Probably one of the most challenging days marking the separation between Joe and me was the day he brought Jen when he picked up the boys. Jen had actually come up to the door. We were civil with each other. I didn't hate Jen, but I was wounded and trying to heal. When I saw her scoop up Max and walk away with my baby in her arms, I wanted to drop to the floor and sink. My grief was so deep; the tears that flooded from my eyes felt as if they awakened the worms buried in the earth. My crippled spirit longed to lie down low in the ground with the creatures that day.

⊞

I was so saturated with sorrow that moment in time. Feelings were difficult for me, but I was realizing that I had not dealt with my emotions for years. I had a lot of work to do in order to deal the deep-rooted grief and hurt that I had stuffed away for so long.

At around the same time, Chelsea, my kitty that I had for years died, at the age of 18. My heartbreak was something I hadn't felt before; she had been a true companion, and I had only been sober for about a year. Chelsea had literally been with me for half my life. I was just leaving my father's home in Potomac when I got Chelsea as a kitten, along with her brother, Sylvester.

Tony and Max were with me when Chelsea was "put down." They were quite young. I believe in my heart that their love for me (and for Chelsea) was so strong that they wanted to say good bye and to be by my side. But I don't think the boys realized the reality, the full scope of what they were going to witness. It was a moment in time for the boys, filled with mystery and grief.

Approximately five or six months later, Nancy told me about a little black kitty she had heard about that needed a home. Tony, Max, and I were excited since all of us loved animals and missed Chelsea. So, we adopted "Mel Gibson."

The boys and I ended up with many animals in the house. Unconsciously, to me it was like keeping the house "alive," especially when Tony and Max were away with Joe. We had a Golden Retriever named Shingi who was not very smart. He failed two training schools, but we loved him dearly, especially Max. Shingi was given this name after Tony and I had watched a documentary about a lion in Africa named Shingalaya. Shingi looked like a tiny lion when we brought him home. In addition to ant farms, Tony had hamsters, birds, and later a snake.

We took trips to the botanical gardens to see the wonderful festive lights during Christmas time, and the butterflies in the spring. How magical it was to be in a large greenhouse filled with Monarch butterflies. When one of the winged beauties would land on the boys, there would be the glimmer in their eyes. These were the most joyous, priceless moments in time. I still remember watching Tony show his little brother how to hold out his finger patiently to allow the Monarch to trust a safe landing. No camera can capture the adoration these brothers had for each other.

On Tony's first day of Kindergarten, I cried watching the bus pull away. He had his little backpack and was so excited. Max and I walked back to the house together and missed big brother Tony.

Tony, Max, and I found a Veterinarian Hospital not far from our house, in the country, where there were sheep, goats, donkeys, geese, ducks, and a few horses in the field. We would drive there regularly and bring them crackers, fruit, and vegetables. As we would pull up, the boys would get excited. The animals would slowly make their way toward us. Some would start to run or move more quickly knowing we were bringing treats. The boys and I would laugh about the smell that would accompany the odd herd.

Max was shy and hesitant. Tony always helped him. There are few photos of them apart from each other. We would go to a petting farm in Virginia where we could hold the baby pigs and bunnies. The boys were so gentle. They laughed so hard when a llama spit on me. I had hay in my hair all day.

Our neighbors, Suzanne and Richard, were an older couple who lived several doors down. I would drink with Richard sometimes in the days that Joe and I were still together, but he was rarely around. The boys and I became close to them as I was going through rehab and then my divorce. Their marriage was the second for each of them. They became like second grandparents to Tony and Max.

We all went to the circus together. Richard was so protective of the boys. To him they were tiny, fragile, and helpless. Richard had grown children, but he was not close to one of his sons. I found out much later that his daughter had committed suicide as a young adult. This seemed to haunt Richard. He and his daughter had fought the day before she took her life. I'm sure whatever words they had weighed heavily on him. He would speak of her on occasion, always fondly. She had jumped off the Chesapeake Bay Bridge, a bridge I crossed often to get to the Eastern Shore.

Staying off the booze and drugs was not the hard part. The difficulty I had was learning how to live as a different person. Neighbors would invite me to have a drink, "just one," and I would decline. People didn't understand that "just one" meant more to me than that. Certainly, I didn't feel the need to explain that I would want eight more and some lines of cocaine too. Drinking was very prevalent where the boys and I lived. We lived out in the country, the boondocks. People would congregate outside their homes and drink. Joe and I used to do it with our friends when he and I were still a couple.

The thing about living where we did was that there were tons of kids residing out in Damascus, which was a bonus for Tony and Max. Many of the county police lived there as well. Slowly, I noticed things like Confederate flags being flown, which didn't really faze me at first.

As I grew more aware of my surroundings, it became clear that racism was prevalent where we lived and neighbors didn't have a problem using the "n" word. It bothered me. There was little diversity at the school where the boys attended, but that wasn't an issue in itself. There were racial issues, such as whispers about the KKK having a presence in the town. Or clerks in the grocery store would openly belly ache about "niggers" in the checkout line. I found this shocking. One night prior to our separation, Joe and I had a party with many our friends. I had a girlfriend from work. She said she was nervous about being there, as she knew there was KKK in our area, and she happened to be black. To me, this was extremely disconcerting. My feelings were conflicted, as I certainly was not raised to believe that there was any race less worthy than mine. But to be honest, I bore a colossal resentment towards the African-American population when I got out of juvenile lock-up; being white there had not worked to my advantage.

These feelings were something I spent many years looking at and coming to peace with. No matter where I ended up, or what predicament I was in, there was always the necessity to look at myself or I could never move on. Despite how I ended up in all those horrible places and what treatment I received, I played a huge part in all of it.

My job at The Adolescent Center was business as usual, but I cannot deny that it was daunting at times. I became extremely close to many of the people I worked with; we were like comrades. Oftentimes we would go out together, attend each other's parties, weddings, showers, and other events.

The individual units that I worked on consisted of a hallway with eight rooms for our male students to reside in. One room had a private bathroom if a student earned the privilege of having this "suite," or if a student needed to be in this space for hygienic reasons.

Our office was at the front of the hallway, which had a door that locked, and a window to the side. All the rooms, including our office, had a small square window in the top, center for safety.

We held weekly staff meetings in our office. There were other, more formal meetings, in the cottage lounges or therapist offices. As a unit, we held daily and weekly meetings with our staff. We also had the boys decompress when they came down from school and process their day.

The year 1998 turned out to be one of several turning points in my career and life. During one of the evening shifts, while we had our unit of boys in the cafeteria for dinner, a fight broke out. Normally, dinner is not eventful—the units keep to themselves, oftentimes the staff is able to socialize with one another to a point, and the residents are well behaved, to a degree. There is some posturing, but they know there is support staff, extra bodies, to handle a crisis.

It happened that on this day we were short staffed, which could often be the case. There were maybe five or six staff members in the cafeteria with more than 18 residents, most of them boys. The potential for a volatile situation was high.

Two of the high school boys started fighting and all the counselors immediately rushed over to break it up. There was no time to strategize what we were going to do or how. Normally, the staff would try to restrain the students until they gained control of themselves. In this case, there were not enough people to restrain both students, and there was always the fear that other residents would get involved. Extra support staff had been called, but it would be a few minutes before they arrived.

Three of us had gone to grab the limbs and torso of one of the boys, who was punching away on the other. Two of the male staff had reached him and had an arm and the other was behind the student. I had gone to grab his other arm. With a force so powerful, without him even looking at me, he thrust my entire body into a column. As if it were in slow motion I recall vividly banging against the concrete, my back hitting the sharp edge and bending like cardboard. I fell down, striking my head against a cafeteria table before I finally hit the ground. Jagged pain surged through my back. It throbbed as I lay helplessly.

Silence. Then yelling, screaming, slamming, banging, and cursing. I heard footsteps and names being called out. Doors opened. Tables slid. Chairs tumbled. Flesh smashed against flesh. Bodies hit the floor. More screaming, slamming, and banging.

The commotion continued. People were saying my name. I tried to get up, but could not. My back felt bruised.

When it was over, after extra staff had arrived to diffuse the situation, several people helped me off the floor. They walked me down to my unit, holding on to me with their arms around my body. I felt extremely fragile.

I went to speak to the residential coordinator, Marcia. She was not a very likable person. Marcia looked at my back and said, "Well, you just have a big red mark on it. I'm sure you will be fine." Everyone, including Marcia, insisted that I go to the hospital to be checked and take several days off if necessary. I was driven to the hospital by one of my fellow unit counselors. Most of us cared a great deal about the well being of each other. People were worried.

The hospital doctor felt that it was a bad contusion and bruised ribs. He wanted me to rest for the week.

In lieu of what happened, my mind thought that if I didn't get back to work soon, I might not want to return at all. I was back within three days.

This was not the last serious incident that occurred at The Adolescent Center that year.

Despite the tumultuous situations that would sometimes arise, I bonded with many young people. Of course, there were always the boundary issues that had to be taken into consideration when working with troubled individuals. When I had become a mother, I felt extremely maternal towards the adolescent boys that were on my unit.

Leon was a 14-year-old African American boy. He lived in Silver Spring with his mother, in theory. Both of his parents were addicted to drugs and I don't think he ever saw his father. His temper was like a wave that would crash down, but he would rarely allow himself to get to the point where staff needed to restrain him. Leon did not like to be touched unless he had control. Deprivation over one's body was a huge issue for many of the kids at The Adolescent Center.

When he was up in the school building, Leon was always in "Alternative Structure," which is where the kids who couldn't handle themselves in the "regular" classroom went, normally due to difficulty with another student, staff, or academics. The classrooms were small and specialized as they were, so Alternative Structure was a tiny room. It was constantly staffed and the students would have harmful objects confiscated.

Leon was about 5'10", and had a thin frame. Realistically, I don't think he ate well when he was at home. I know he had started getting high a lot with buddies and was dealing on the streets.

The mid 1990's were when kids started wearing their jeans down past their briefs. We could always see Leon's undergarments. I never thought it was a good look. Leon looked older, which was to his detriment. This was the case for many of the larger kids. So many of these youth grew up fast, and they would never get their innocence back.

Leon would often suck his thumb. This was not unusual for many of the adolescents that were at The Adolescent Center. Often when he did this, he also liked to hold a special stuffed animal. It was so old and raggedy; you couldn't surmise what it originally was. In many ways, Leon was just a young child in a big body.

When the weekends rolled around for him to go home, his mom would usually come late. But he was one of the lucky ones, at least she came regularly.

At Christmas time, Leon would go home as most of the kids did. Sadly, that one year that he was with us, Leon brought back a television guide that he said he had gotten as a gift. Whether that was the entire truth or not, it seemed devastating to me. I knew Leon did not get much from his mother. Drugs were her priority.

Leon had such an attitude. He didn't care about the cops, staff, or teachers. He had a tough situation.

We would play cards at night on the unit, usually Rummy 500. Leon would laugh at silly jokes. Despite him being a bit of a thug, I was able to find something likable about him, and he sensed that. My co-worker Jennifer was also able to humor him. He knew it was genuine. It didn't matter to him that I was staff at The Adolescent Center or that I was white. Trust with authority and across races was big with these kids. They had been through tragic ordeals. I got it. Sure there were times when he would get belligerent with me, but for the most part, we were able to have a respectful relationship. He knew that I had a job to do, and I knew that it was arduous for him to be stuck on a residential unit. Of course, Leon did often talk about getting high. This was a coping mechanism.

Amusingly, Leon would be humored when he was told it was time to have our unit meetings or retire for the evening. He enjoyed rebelling. But Leon would joke, "OK, Trisha, I don't like it when you give me those evil eyes. I will go."

"You scare me Trisha!" he would say. "I don't want you pissed at me." He would use sarcastic humor, me with my 5'5 frame weighing about 105 pounds at the time.

"You a witch with that blonde hair," he would say, as he would give his giggly laugh with his big pearly whites.

There were certain people that he didn't want to disappoint, and he would listen to them. I knew I was one of those people. I never abused his trust.

One day Leon had a crushingly volatile day in school and was in Alternative Structure. I had gotten a call from the school, as my staff (residential) would "man" the room if we were able to during our shift. When I had gotten to Leon that morning, he was inconsolable. Gradually, he talked to me about issues at home.

I don't know if what was going on with him that day was the truth. I remember talking to the therapist about his situation. She knew that possibly it was difficult for me to filter what Leon would say to me. I think she knew that he trusted me, and that I was able to comfort him to a certain degree, but that Leon was a bona-fide manipulator.

Leon asked me to bring my pink sweater to him. I wore it a lot on the unit. He was cold in the Alternative Structure room. It was the least I could do for him that day. I went down to the residential unit and brought the soft sweater to him that he requested. For hours, he kept himself bundled in my large, fluffy, bright pink sweater. Somehow, it calmed him.

Another young man that left an impression on me, and on many of the other staff members, was Ryan. Ryan originally had been placed on a unit in another building. He was there for months and we often discussed him in our staff strategy meetings with all the other team members. His unit staff seemed frustrated with Ryan. He was out of control often, and was being restrained and safety coated on a regular basis. When this happened, it involved extra staff and layers of documentation.

My unit coordinator requested that Ryan be transferred to us, which was unusual. Possibly a different therapeutic milieu could have a positive impact on him was our thinking. Ryan's history, particularly with his mom, was gloomy and absurd. To know what happened to many of the young people broke our hearts. It was almost impossible to fathom. The way Ryan would describe his ordeals couldn't be made up. Ryan's anger stemmed from the fact that he couldn't be at home and he was baffled as to why he had been removed.

Ryan would speak of his mother hitting him in the head with a baseball bat. Once, he tried to get some help at a fair because his head was bleeding. Blood was spilling down his face, into his eyes and he couldn't see very well. Somehow the police were alerted to Ryan and this is how he and his family got further involved in the legal system. This was not the first incident with Ryan and his mother. But the thing about him is, he didn't want to leave his mom. His loyalty to her was unwavering.

He was 14 years old, white, and about 5'9. He was very thin and had brown, soft eyes. When you got to know him, there was not an evil, cruel bone in his body. Ryan was deeply emotionally wounded. When Ryan got to our unit he was hyper and combative. His normal behavior was to test limits and staff. Initially, Ryan needed to be restrained and safety coated regularly. He cried out for attention, and sometimes it was impossible to provide all that he needed. The funny thing about Ryan was he would not curse or get violent towards us. So when he would get out of control and we couldn't calm him with words or limits, Ryan would say humorous things. We had one staff on our unit who Ryan had a love/hate relationship with, Paul. Though he was about 6'3" in stature, Paul had a very gentle spirit. Ryan would call out to him, "Ya Big Tall Tree! Get your hands off me!"

Dear God, as we all tried to calm this out of control adolescent in crisis and he would blurt out these remarks, it was difficult not to smirk. When he was able to settle into a routine and know that he could trust some folks, things changed dramatically for Ryan.

He never went home on weekends, and we did not meet his mother. For months and months, Ryan was hopeful that she would call and that there would be a connection. He would amp himself up each weekend. Sadly for him, it never happened while he resided with us at The Adolescent Center. Ryan would go through a plethora of emotions, but had no clue how his behavior was associated with his situation.

The staff on my unit adored Ryan when he was able to maintain some calmness. Eventually, he was able to progress through school and create some trusting relationships with peers and staff. Ryan became a model student, but we knew he needed to move on. We felt it was best to look into another living situation for him beyond The Adolescent Center, as it seemed apparent he would not return home.

Ryan went to a Forestry Camp in Winchester, Virginia, that was suited to seriously emotionally disturbed adolescent boys. The philosophy of their treatment was to treat the "whole boy" on many levels. He took advantage of any help he could get and thrived from the experience.

Four of us who worked with Ryan on the unit at The Adolescent Center went to visit him in Winchester. I brought Tony. Some of the boys that I worked with knew Tony. They were oddly bridged together.

Ryan could not have been more touched by us trekking out to see him. He was in tears. We brought little gifts to make it special, as we knew he didn't have much where he was. Ryan took pride in showing us the grounds where he resided and how the program operated. It was rigorous. He had been successful and continued to impress us. He was thrilled to see us all, including Tony. My beautiful memory from the day was when Ryan held Tony and put him up on his shoulders. The two of them were such lights in my life—Tony from my womb, and Ryan from the facility where we tried and hopefully succeeded to nurture him and give him a better life.

Ryan was eventually able to get out on his own from the Forestry Camp. He became a volunteer firefighter.

I was still working my two sixteen-hour shifts and one regular to make my forty hours. By this time I had adjusted to my schedule and was managing, even thought it was a tough time with sobriety, a stressful job, and divorce. My boys were such an inspiration They were celestial beings in my life that kept me afloat, and there is no other way to describe how much they meant.

TWENTY FIVE

had never predicted myself living a typical life, but somehow I did Raising two boys and watching them grow was a gift.

Every year that I would attend Tony and Max's teacher conferences, I would cry. The news was always so bright and positive—how polite they were, how smart and dedicated to their schoolwork they were. The boys were sociable and had other kids gravitate to them. They were perfect in my eyes.

Tony and Max would walk to school in the morning with their friends, along a path that wove through the neighborhood. I would try and meet them on the way home, along with Shingi, our beloved Golden Retriever. This was such a delight for all of us.

Joe and I had odd hours and continued to manipulate our schedules so that childcare was not a weighing issue. For a period of time, the boys would go with my sister Sheila. Normally, one of us would drop them off at Sheila's house about thirty minutes north of us, and I would pick them up around 11:30 p.m. They would be asleep. This was not ideal as hours go, but the boys were precious to Sheila.

Sheila and her husband Bob's two daughters, Heather and Emily, adored Tony and Max. They lived in a cozy log cabin that they had built themselves on twelve acres of land atop a steep hill in Mt. Airy, Maryland.

Bob loved the boys and was always playing with them when he had the energy after a long day at work. I will never forget one particular snowy evening coming up the driveway. My recollection is that I barely made it to the top. The ice and snow were fresh. As usual, Sheila greeted me at the door. She was so gentle and obliging. Bob must have been looking out the window or had been at the door himself. He came running out to us and was yelling. The car had started rolling down the hill. It must have been slippery enough that the tires had no grip. Bob jumped in the driver's seat and maneuvered the car back up the hill. Sheila and I just stood there stunned for a few moments. I was relieved my car didn't go tumbling in to the woods or speed down the hill and on to the street, goodness. Bob was my hero that night. Sheila was my hero every day for years.

We always chatted for a few moments and Sheila would give me a report about the boys. I would scoop them up and be on my way. That evening, I felt especially grateful.

It seemed that work and the boys were my life, and I was content with this. I got sober for them. But I would get little reminders from people in my life or counselors that it was crucial I stay clean for myself. My recovery took a back seat to the boys for a long time. They were everything, my lifeline. I was a mother. I also needed to work and support them.

I found my work with the kids at The Adolescent Center extremely gratifying. I had come full circle in multiple ways. There was a reason I came to be a counselor on a unit at this place. On many levels, I understood what these kids were going through, and what they were fighting about. Funny, I didn't picture my family "troubled" like the families I worked with, but I understood the despair and anger that they were going through that was the result of a struggle. We all come to it in different ways.

There were moments when I became acutely aware of the instincts that I was raised with. For instance, as I was beginning to raise Tony, and Max was still an infant, I would spank Tony's bottom out of anger or lack of patience. Somehow, this didn't feel like adequate child rearing. Joe and I talked about it and agreed that physical discipline was not an option for either of us, whether we were together or not. So, I would use "time outs" for Tony and Max instead. That usually sufficed if I had problems with them not listening. Often I would joke about using bribery or threats with the boys, as I found that I could entice them as well with treats or take things away temporarily if they didn't listen. In retrospect, it was usually if I was having a bad day or if the boys weren't active enough that would make for chaos in the house.

Occasionally, we would take vacations together.

Once, my Dad and Sharon took us to Disney World, as they did for my sisters and their families. The boys and I went in November 2000, right after Thanksgiving when Al Gore had lost his bid for the Presidency. This was the first plane ride for Tony and Max. I remember we were sitting at the airport, waiting to board, when Joe came to see us off. He was thrilled to see the boys go on an adventure into the sky and off to Disney! The flight attendants gave Tony and Max little pins indicating that they were "first time flyers." These were special tokens for the boys at that moment. Tony and Max had no fear of going into the air on a big airplane; they were elated.

My memory of my father and the boys with him is special. I don't know if my father went to places like Disney World when he was younger. To see him experience this with his grandchildren was magical. The theme at the time was the Scrooge, as the movie had just come out with Jim Carrey. Scrooge paraphernalia was everywhere!

Dad rode the spinning teacups and the kids' rollercoaster with the boys. He laughed hysterically. I screamed. I wanted to vomit in those teacups. He seemed to enjoy going on each ride just as much as the boys did. It was like watching a grown child, a side I had not seen in my father.

We ended up going to Magic Kingdom, Sea World, and Animal Kingdom. The boys always had such a love and appreciation for animals, as did Sharon and my father. Poor Max! One day he was trying to feed the seals when a bird dove down and stole the food right out of his hand. He cried, but we went back and got more food for him to give the squealing seals. All of us then sat and caressed the huge manta rays as they swam beside the side of the tank to us. How sleek they felt. The boys were so gentle and respectful.

At night, Dad would teach the boys how to play poker in the hotel. Joe and I would laugh about that on the phone when he would call to check in with Tony and Max. The boys appreciated what a generous gesture it was that my father and Sharon took us on this trip. There were rides, little safaris, games, time with the animals, and treks through all the parks that bonded all of us. The boys always knew to say "thank you." They knew that this was the proper thing to say when someone did something kind.

Tony in his football uniform.

My isolation and the fight to stay sober were masked by my determination to raise Tony and Max as best I could. For them to know that they were loved and wanted was crucial. The boys flourished in school and had many friends. They enjoyed our day trips to the zoo, museums carnivals, and other places. We loved outings together and they soaked in the world around them.

For a while, Joe and I tried to keep things as normal as possible and do holidays together, but our hearts were too far apart. We both adored Tony and Max, but we had become disconnected. I "allowed" Joe to interfere with my serenity in that I knew I could not control him or his actions. But I also knew that he did the best he could. It was less complicated for Joe if he could be available a few days a week. But even then, he would cancel at times. This frustrated me, but there was also a part of me that was comforted by my time alone with the boys. They saved my life.

Max, early soccer player.

How I loved watching Max run up and down the soccer field once he decided this was his sport. And Tony, weighed down with the entire padding, helmet, and other various gear in the 100-degree summer heat, to be a football player with the best of them in Damascus. He played soccer and baseball as well. It took him years to find what his real niche was. There were not many practices or games that I missed. It was a delight to watch the boys in their element. I took such pride in making sure their gear was clean, that I participated as best I could to get other players to practice if possible, bring snacks for all the other boys and girls, made calls when asked, and help out in whatever way I could as a sports mother.

I would discover that as a mother of active boys, there would be numerous trips to the hospital emergency room.

Tony was the first to make the trip.

The boys would regularly play out in front of the townhouse where I could sit on the step and watch over them. Normally, they would ride tricycles, blow bubbles, draw with chalk on the sidewalk, or play ball with friends. There was always a gathering of other boys and girls from the neighborhood.

Our townhome was on an incline. Tony would start at the top of the hill and ride his little Big Wheel from the top with giggles and exuberance. One sunny day, Tony had come flying down with that glorious gleam in his eye. He lost control and flipped about three times. I could tell he was hurt. Tony immediately looked to me. I ran down to him and called out his name. "Tony, Tony, my sweetie, are you OK?" He first whimpered and then broke out in to tears. I scooped him up and brought him into the house. I was so relieved I had Tony wear a helmet. He hurt his shoulder. At the time, I didn't know it was broken. He was so calm and genteel. He fell asleep on the couch. I thought Tony just banged himself up and was shaken. The next day, he had trouble with his shoulder and obviously in pain. I called the doctor. He said for us to go to the emergency room and have Tony checked out.

When we found out that Tony broke his collarbone I wondered how I couldn't have known right away. What a terrible mother I felt like.

Max was next—times two.

The first time Max had to go was when we had family over on the back deck for a cookout. Max was probably a mere two or three year old. He would lie with Shingi and hug him regularly, which was tolerated by our sweet family dog. Max happened to very imprudently step on Shingi's tail, completely unaware of what he had done. Shingi snapped. The reaction was so swift; I couldn't have gotten there quickly enough. The dog bit Max in the face, right below his eye. First there was a gasp from my mouth, I'm sure. Max appeared to be fine. Then the blood came. My impulse was to smack the hell out of Shingi. He never touched the boys aggressively again.

Off to the hospital we went. Max got a Popsicle rather than stitches. Shingi was up on all his shots, so no needles needed for Max. He still has a little scar under his eye from the dog bite.

The next trip happened one day at the pool, during joyful hours of catching Max jumping in from the side.

In the summers, we were at the pool almost daily. Tony and Max always had friends they were playing with. As a youngster, Max clung to me; he was affectionate and I never grew weary of him wanting to be held. Max soaked up intense delight when he would jump in to my arms from the edge of the pool and I would catch him. He could do it all day, and there would be endless laughter and giggles. I would twirl him around in the water and smooch his tummy.

I had a pair of sunglasses on in the pool that day. At one point Max jumped to me and couldn't see that I wasn't looking. My arms weren't held out to retrieve him safely. His chin banged into my head. Max bit down on to his tongue. I didn't catch him. Immediately there was silence, blood, and then tears.

I quickly lifted him out of the water. Max had a huge gash, rather a hole through his tongue that was bleeding profusely. The lifeguards offered me paper towels to assist in stopping the bleeding. I grappled with the inefficiency of how unprepared for an emergency they were, but needed to focus on Max. I asked them to call 911.

There was little the hospital could do, as wounds in the mouth are difficult to treat, apparently, due to germs and moisture. Basically Max would need to rinse with baking soda and we were given antibiotics for possible infection. For several months he had a gaping scar and a flap of flesh that he would stick out and show off to people

217

when they asked about his incident. He was probably four years old at the time.

Both boys ended up going to the emergency room from rollerblade falls. The trail that rolled through our development was wonderful for them to ride their bikes, rollerblades, and skateboards, but it was treacherous.

Max was with Tony and four or five other friends one day, rollerblading. I was not far behind him on the sidewalk, but he was out of my sight. He turned a corner ahead of me. I didn't see him take the fall, but I knew when he came at me with the bloody chin that it wasn't good. He never screamed out with pain, but the gash on his face was bad. For some reason, boys liked to show the wound, every detail. As Max was awaiting his trip to the hospital, he would spread open the two sides of the flesh only to expose more tissue and blood. I personally found it nauseating. The reaction of the other kids was always entertaining, they all liked to make sure he was OK, but gawk at the meaty wound just for kicks.

This particular trip was interesting in that I always needed to maintain my composure for the boys during a crisis or emergency. Max was put on a gurney and needed stitches. Together we held numbing cream and ice on his face. Before they needed to stitch him up, Max was wrapped in a papoose so he wouldn't try to grab at the nurse or doctor. Apparently, it was standard procedure but not pleasant for him or me as the parent. The physician came to stitch him up. I watched. Big mistake. This was a cardinal rule that I kept, always: Never looked at needles, doctor's instruments, or anything like that. I felt that if I did, then fear would set in. That day at the hospital when I looked at the needle that was going in to my son's wounded rawness, and his innocent eyes peered up at me, it was too much for me to handle. I became faint. The nurse saw I was turning white. She asked if I wanted to lie next to Max. Yes, I needed to. We both got popsicles that day.

Tony took a bad fall off his rollerblades a few years later.

My neighbors Suzanne, Rick, and I were walking on the trail with the dogs. By this time, I had another dog, Sadie. She was such a dear, half Shar-pei and Chow. The boys loved her just as much. We were family.

Tony was at the top of a large hill and started coming down. Rick was nervous about him skating down. "Will he be OK?"

"Trisha, that hill is steep, he may lose control. How will he be able to brake?"

I very confidently replied, "Rick, he will be fine."

Tony started coming, rolling with the usual chuckle. His speed picked up. He was going too fast. I could tell he could not control the speed or be able to stop. I will never forget the look of terror in Tony's eyes that day. He lunged down the hill and plunged on to the pavement face first.

The first yell came from Rick.

"Oh my God, that was a horrible fall that he took!" We all went running to Tony who was also in distress. As he came toward me, I could see that Tony not only had bloody lips, but there was something off with his teeth. Oh no!! His two front teeth were not looking good. He had chipped both of his beautiful upper incisors practically in half. Tony was in tears. Rick, who was probably about 65 at the time, carried him to our home, rollerblades and all.

Tony was inconsolable. I had made an emergency appointment with our dentist. Tony's teeth were in bad shape, and he needed to get somewhere urgently. One tooth had broken almost all the way down to his gums. What I had deciphered from Tony is that he was thinking in his head they would be like that forever. It was important he understand we could get them repaired, and he would be OK.

We got to the dentist and Tony was seen. It seemed that I didn't fill out the proper paperwork that year to add dental insurance for the boys and me. Tony obviously needed specialized dental work. After many phone calls with Joe, and finding out that my mom had a wonderful dentist who would do a phenomenal job on Tony, knowing it was an emergency, we were able to get him the care that he needed. Joe paid cash for it up front.

⌘

This was a substantial moment in my separated life from Joe. It was crucial that I understand he would rise to the occasion for the boys. There was absolutely no doubt that there were and would be moments that Joe drove me to anger that could not be measured. The pain I felt for the boys and I went to a sphere in my soul that would drop me to the earth like a crumply leaf. But when Joe would step up and do something as generous as pay out of his pocket for Tony to get his teeth fixed, it meant a great deal. He would come through this way for many years. To me, it was a reminder of his amazing character and why I married him in the first place.

There was a softening that began for me at that moment. I was able to find compassion and forgiveness for a man I once truly loved. I realized that in spite of the disconnection that I felt from Joe, he was the father of my children. I realized that he would be in my life forever, in some capacity. Tony and Max bonded us. I knew in my heart that Joe loved the boys, and that he just showed it differently.

I suppose for me the question became, how on earth could I protect my angels? Nothing else mattered. But at some point, I had to make a decision regarding other aspects of my life, such as my recovery. If not, then I couldn't be a well-balanced friend, mother, worker, or anything else.

As time went on, people would say, "Trish, get a life!" In my mind, Tony and Max were my life. Didn't they understand? In some ways this was a warning.

TWENTY SIX

Raising two boys as a single mother, I had returned to work full time. I also went back to school, which had never been my forte. Each paper, exam, and class took great effort. I lacked the same zeal that I had possessed when I first set out to get my college education years ago.

But how could I be a role model to my boys if I haven't even graduated from college? Tony and Max were always told from a young age they would go and this was something Joe and I agreed on no matter what.

It took me a few years, but I earned my Bachelor's degree. It was a big deal to me because I had come so close to finishing when Joe and I married. I also had to work hard when it came to academics, considering my difficulties in high school

Mom took me on a trip as a graduation gift. It was the first trip on my own since the boys were born. We went to Sea World, but the best part of the trip included us swimming with dolphins and spending a whole day with them in Florida. I was ecstatic. Mom and I were like two besties on the flight down. We talked and chuckled about this wonderful adventure we were undertaking, and how it was reminiscent of the old days traveling back and forth somehow. I loved the warm air and palm trees that we flew to when we dropped down into Orlando.

There was something mystical about dolphins. They seem to be acutely aware of humans and how they have confined them in captivity. I suppose some time later I had some feelings about all creatures being exploited in such a way. But at the time I was thrilled just to be in the water with these beautiful mammals. I held onto one of the stunning fellows while he rocketed through the blue water and dove to the bottom of the huge enclosure, with me holding his flipper. Somehow, I was the only one in the group permitted to do this. I asked if I could have more time with the dolphins.

Mom and I hung out in the dolphin cove all day. We swam with the rays, as well. It wasn't the same, but it was still magnificent. To be able to have this experience with my mother was such an extreme departure from my teenage days. It was difficult for me to imagine that time. The two of us had come so far. For us to be able to freely enjoy each other's company, talk about what was happening in our lives, laugh, giggle, and share this incredible encounter together would have been unheard of years ago.

Up until that point I hadn't taken good care of my health or appearance. Many things had changed once I was clean and sober—the boys were well dressed and always had magnificent toys to keep them entertained, but somehow I had lost myself in my parenting.

I started caring for my outward appearance and taking more pride in myself. Inwardly, I was feeling more positive about myself and it seemed to be a reflection of what I wanted to show the world.

Dating was a whole new realm with sobriety and the new tech age. I fumbled around with this strange world to find a possible companion. Though I had been worldly, gone to college, had children, and had even lived on the streets, dating was agonizing. How could I be so unknowing of men and relationships?

It seemed that being a non-drinker made me a bit of an anomaly. I may have come across as insecure as well. Sometimes, the person was more interested in me than I was for him, or vice versa. Unfortunately, the crevices of my memory still contained remnants of a very disconnected way to be with the opposite sex. My past still felt like such a curse.

I hadn't learned early on in life that an emotional connection with a man was far more important than a physical one. I found it challenging to build a lasting relationship. Memories of acts from my addictions spun through my mind, and warped behavior that I had taken part in while I was high. The extent to which my essence and emotions were still damaged was apparent. I had much work to do inside. I hadn't had a drink or a drug in a while, but really I had no quality recovery. It was important that Tony and Max no longer be the constant spotlight of my life. I had to be with other alcoholics, and to reach out to them so that I would not forget how desperate I had once been. I never wanted to go back to the bondage of addiction. I had to stop hiding behind the boys and my dysfunctional behavior.

It took years to build real friendships and enjoy the company of sober, genuine people. Interestingly Carol, my dear little sister, and I, became very close, and would get together almost weekly for several years. During my drinking and using days, Carol and I sometimes would go to the bars downtown together. I loved flirting with the men and dancing to the music. Carol and I would have a blast getting some energy out dancing to the latest music at the wild clubs. We had gut-busting laughter nights that we will never forget. But there were evenings that were lonely and empty for both of us. In many ways, we were yearning for something that we were never going to find in those twisted, perverse joints. For me, the elixirs that once brought me joy and numbness had stopped working years before. I had to use so many more substances to get the thumping to leave my brain. It never worked.

When I got clean, Carol and I found healthy activities to do together, like hiking or biking on the canal. We would go to brunch in Georgetown. She and I shared the sadness of missing Greece, and not many people could relate. Later, Carol would discover a whole world called Third Culture Kids that would describe us. But it didn't take away the pain. We would go to Greek Festivals together and often Sheila, Nancy, and Mom or Dad would join us. The music, food and people were such fun to partake in. Often, we would run into someone that we knew from overseas.

To have and share precious moments with my family was something I could not have imagined as a teenager during my struggling years. Part of working a recovery program was looking at me, walking through fears and resentment, and making amends to those people I had harmed in my past. I told my parents and sisters how sorry I was for all the difficulty I had caused. These were not easy conversations.

I particularly remember approaching my mother. I recall precisely which room we were in, in the house on Carvel Street, where Mom lived with Miranda. She said, "Patricia, you could have ended up hard. But you didn't. After everything you have been through, I commend you for the changes you have been able to make." Coming from Mom, and all she and I had been through, despite my unsettled demons, I had been able to soften a bit. Thank God.

It was crucial that I clear away the past and start anew. When I spoke to my father, we were on a family trip to Bethany Beach, Delaware. I told Sharon that I wanted to speak to him privately and she understood. Dad and I walked around town window-shopping. I was nervous.

"Dad," I said. "I know that when I was younger there were many things I did that were difficult for you to deal with."

He looked at me and listened. We were sitting in the Frog House Family Restaurant, a bit of a dive.

I started getting teary, but I wanted to be clear with my words.

"Dad, I am so sorry for all the damage I caused when I was a teenager. I know it was hurtful for you and Mom."

He took my hand. He smiled.

"Trisha, the past is in the past. I don't think about it."

He continued, "I am so proud of the work you have done. I know it hasn't been easy for you, and you have done an incredible job with the boys."

We did not say much more. It did not seem necessary.

My father had a way of being brief about such matters.

How thankful and truly aware I was that I had an actual relationship with my mother and father after all we had been through! There were some Christmases when the piles of presents would be stacked halfway up the tree. Tony, Max, and their cousins would play and giggle into the late hours of the night, always entertaining the adults, who had somehow forgotten what youth was all about. There were many such memorable holidays with the whole family.

Early into my sobriety and separation from Joe, I had to work one Thanksgiving. But my family waited to celebrate until I could join them later that afternoon. As I drove over in solitude and glanced in strangers' windows, it felt as though everyone except me was happy. Surely, no one else could feel as grief stricken.

When I got to my father's house, I felt a deep sorrow. The boys were with Joe. My mood was low. I remember being teary when I got to the house. My sisters and Sharon were already preparing dinner. It was going to be an effort for me to celebrate this holiday.

Dad said, "Trisha would you like to go for a walk before dinner?"

It was chilly, the sky was grey, and there was a familiar, smoky fragrance that I loved—the smell of burning wood in a fireplace that crept into the neighborhood air. I shared with Dad what I was thinking on the way over. The emptiness and sadness was hard to describe, but obviously apparent.

Dad said, "Trish, when your Mom left I felt that way too. I understand."

This was an extremely rare moment in time with my father; he did not talk about feelings often, if at all. For him to relate to how I could feel made me feel some relief on that frigid evening in Virginia.

He held my hand for a few minutes as we walked. My father did this on occasion. We would be some place together and he would reach out for my hand or give me a pat on the shoulder acknowledging affection.

I felt so comforted and secure. My mood softened.

I felt the warmth of my family, the people I had not been able to express affection towards for years. I didn't wish to be anywhere but with my loved ones. Of course, I longed to have the boys with me, but it was important for them to celebrate with Joe as well.

Dinner with my family was festive. We shared stories from celebrations of earlier days. Dad told the best jokes. Mom brought Miranda and we all chimed in to tell the best story of past years or other family gatherings. There were always humorous moments that everyone could bust up about. The laughter that would fill the room was contagious.

That evening was a revelation. Knowing that I could shift my mood, my attitude, and enjoy the moment and the company, was significant in my transformation. I could have been miserable, but I chose instead to dig deep into my spirit. This was new. I didn't get sober to lead a miserable life. I owed it to the boys and those around me to try and be a happy person.

TWENTY SEVEN

It had been pointed out to me that I could not love anyone during the times I was a rebellious adolescent. It was as if I had no capacity to feel when I was in a haze. I was so filled with rage that it was all I could do to be out there running and getting my booze and drugs, fighting the world.

When Tony and Max came along, somehow love had swayed my demeanor. Nothing else existed. The fact that I could get clean while they were still young was a gift. I met women and men who lost their children due to the disease. Hearing stories of the ones who continued to use and drink throughout their kids' lives, and listening to them talk about the guilt and remorse they felt, made me grateful indeed. I don't know if I could have lived with putting Tony and Max through a lifetime of my use.

In many ways, I had defied the odds. To a system that had wanted to give up on me years and years ago, I had been such an indisputable success story. My parents and sisters never gave up on me, and I rebuilt bonds with them while creating a family of my own. Somehow, I had come to peace with all the running and fighting. It churned and twisted like a hurricane inside, but that was the thing about recovery—you had to brave all that life put in front of you. There was always the residue of the damage from behind.

I faced negative odds when it came to my success in sobriety, as well. In the outpatient rehab, they did not have a good outlook for me either. There were the chronic relapsers and others who didn't recover. I felt so blessed to have survived what I had been through, and to be given a second chance to get my life in order.

I could not allow my fate to determine my faith. I knew that I would always be OK, as long as I tried to do the right thing. I plodded along, doing what I could to have quality recovery. Some days were a delight, others not so much. But the days that didn't go my way allowed me to appreciate the good and joyous moments that did come along. I came to know that life is precious. I tried so tenderly to meet each person where they were on their journey in life.

It was virtually impossible for me to not realize how far I had come, from the teenager who acted out and ran away to the responsible, caring parent who was sober and trying to help troubled youth. I was not able to credit myself with the work it took to get sober. It never occurred to me that I had literally morphed from a married woman with no self-esteem to a feisty, single mother, raising two young boys with values and perspective that would allow them their own freedoms.

I found that trust was such an uncharted territory. In my mind, everyone would leave, or hurt me in the end. I suppose, in some distorted way, I had deluded myself thinking that Tony and Max would never leave. But if I wanted them to be normal young men, as they grew older, it was important for me to give them the sufficient emotional and physical support they needed. They would need to fly on their own one day. My hope was that we would be close to each other or see one another often wherever we all were.

Would I ever imagine my life to be what it had become? Not in a million years! If anyone had asked me about my work, husband, my exquisite boys, and the ability to reconnect with family, I wouldn't have even created such gifts for myself.

I didn't have to look back, despite the fact that I felt affected by the psych ward and all I had seen and experienced there, like the withered gentleman who tried taking his life by blasting a bullet through his mouth, and the woman who would come squawking into my room at night with her lonely tales and stubs hanging from the wheelchair. All the different characters will remain etched in my mind.

Eventually, I was able to find my friend Hannah, the one whom I went AWOL with from Shepherd Place. She and I reminisced and laughed about events from years earlier. She was only thirteen when we were in Shepherd Place together. I never knew this when we ran that day. Afterwards, she nearly died on many occasions, she said, because she was a junkie. I pictured her in cars, nearly dead on the streets of Baltimore or D.C., chasing her fix, or in a hospital room, with doctors trying to resuscitate her.

Hannah had also been sent to Montrose from Shepherd Place. Or as my friend Christine would say, "She got the Montrose card."

As we shared our stories, she quietly told me her tale, and I gave her mine. It was with a heavy heart that I listened to her purge the torment she went through at Montrose.

Hannah had been stuck in isolation over a snowy weekend. She had tried running from Montrose too, and got thrown in an isolation room for days. There was no changing of the guards due to the horrendous weather. The man who was watching over her, the guard, the state appointed official, raped her repeatedly for three days. Over and over again, my friend was violently, sexually exploited by a man who was supposed to be vigilant in his care. My heart bled, my head hurt, and my veins swelled as Hannah told me this. How? Why?

But there was a part of me that was calm and unsurprised. I knew Montrose. It was such a nightmare.

Hannah confidently said, "I'm OK Trisha. I had a lot of therapy through the years to deal with it."

I believed her and it was true. She had gotten off the drugs and made a better life for herself. Hannah was one of the odd few as well. But I knew that she carried those scars somewhere inside. They don't go away. We all have them, some worse than others.

Heroin would have been devastating for me, given the power of my addictions. It would have ravaged me more than the coke, weed, and booze combined. But somehow I had been saved from this dreadful drug. I thank my God.

How could I forget all the moments that led me to the trouble and havoc: The times sleeping out in the cold woods, the abandoned houses, ending up with dealers, thugs and gangs, until my eventual demise at the hotel with police blasting the doors down and guns pointed in my face? But through all the hardship what clung to my spirit, the most were the multiple lock-ups in Baltimore.

I had felt so doomed when I first took in the sights, players, smells, overseers, metal bars, and the thought of time lost and freedom taken away. Montrose, rather the time I had spent there, had emotionally chiseled away at my very being. I wanted to expunge this place from my soul. That period of my life had impacted many aspects of who I had become. I'm sure my anger was a part of my drug and alcohol use. Once the elixir, white powder, and weed were gone, my rage manifested itself everywhere, especially in my relationships. My marriage never had a chance. It was impossible for me to have any healthy relationship with myself or another human being unless I could take a hard look at my past, and somehow move forward.

This is where the acceptance piece was crucial. I realized that I was unique and special in many ways, and that I had gifts to give. I didn't have to be a problem in society; I could be a contribution. My literal fight to endure life somehow allowed me to come out OK. There was much rebuilding and work repairing of damage that I had done through the years. But there could be no healing, unless there was some sort of awareness of the pain.

I could not continue to let my heart be crippled by brokenness and the gloom of the past. Somehow, my tears would transpire into joy and hope if I kept my heart open and was determined in faith. Knowing that the boys and I were watched over gave me solace and comfort. One day we would all fly, even my Tony and Max.

My final thoughts are of freedom, of course. One of my favorite authors, Kahlil Gibran, wrote:

You shall be free indeed when your days are not without a care nor your thoughts without a want and a grief,

But rather when these things girdle your life and yet you rise above them naked and unbound.

And how shall you rise beyond your days and nights unless you break the chains which you at the dawn of your understanding have fastened around your noon hour?

In truth that which you call freedom is the strongest of these chains, though its links glitter in the sun and dazzle your eyes.

I was free from the bondage of addiction that struck me like a bolt from the underworld. And now, somehow, I could search for a glimmer of that golden blonde girl who once joyously ran through the poppy fields in the place that she adored as her home.

With my beloved boys Tony and Max.